William Shakespeare (bapt. 26 April 1564 – 23 April 1616) was an English poet, playwright and actor, widely regarded as the greatest writer in the English language and the world's greatest dramatist. He is often called England's national poet and the "Bard of Avon". His extant works, including collaborations, consist of approximately 39 plays, 154 sonnets, two long narrative poems, and a few other verses, some of uncertain authorship. His plays have been translated into every major living language and are performed more often than those of any other playwright. Shakespeare was born and raised in Stratford-upon-Avon, Warwickshire. At the age of 18, he married Anne Hathaway, with whom he had three children: Susanna and twins Hamnet and Judith. Sometime between 1585 and 1592, he began a successful career in London as an actor, writer, and part-owner of a playing company called the Lord Chamberlain's Men, later known as the King's Men. At age 49 (around 1613), he appears to have retired to Stratford, where he died three years later. (Source: Wikipedia)

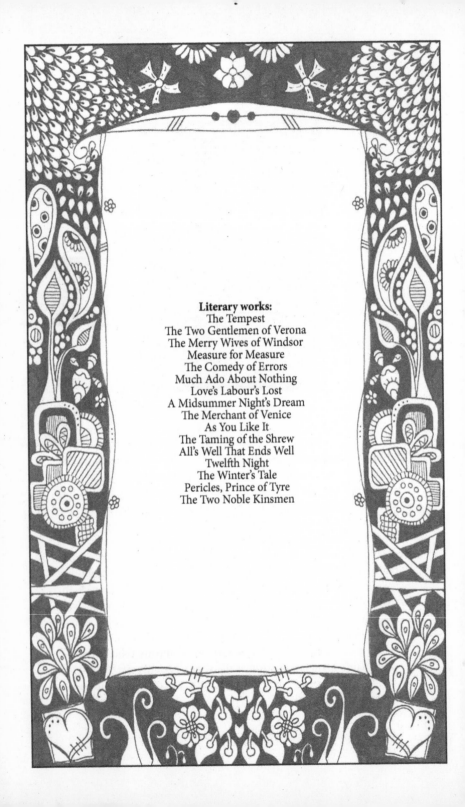

Literary works:
The Tempest
The Two Gentlemen of Verona
The Merry Wives of Windsor
Measure for Measure
The Comedy of Errors
Much Ado About Nothing
Love's Labour's Lost
A Midsummer Night's Dream
The Merchant of Venice
As You Like It
The Taming of the Shrew
All's Well That Ends Well
Twelfth Night
The Winter's Tale
Pericles, Prince of Tyre
The Two Noble Kinsmen

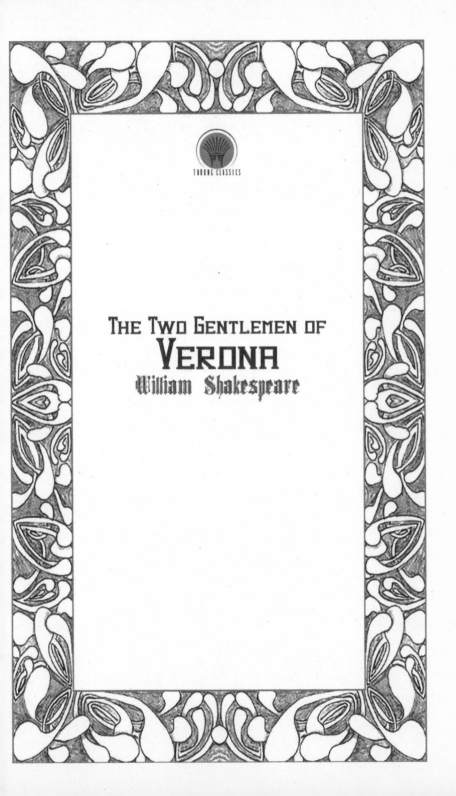

THRONG CLASSICS

The Two Gentlemen of
VERONA
William Shakespeare

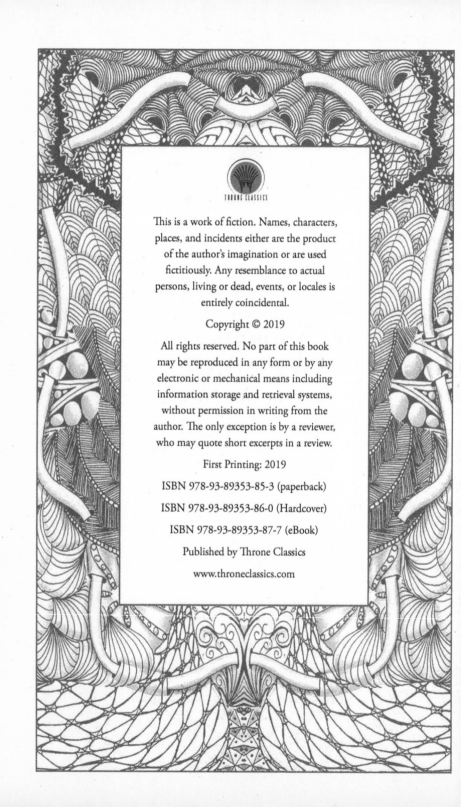

First Printing: 2019

ISBN 978-93-89353-85-3 (paperback)

ISBN 978-93-89353-86-0 (Hardcover)

ISBN 978-93-89353-87-7 (eBook)

Published by Throne Classics

www.throneclassics.com

Contents

THE TWO GENTLEMEN OF
VERONA

DRAMATIS PERSONAE

DUKE OF MILAN, father to Silvia

VALENTINE, one of the two gentlemen

PROTEUS, one of the two gentlemen

ANTONIO, father to Proteus

THURIO, a foolish rival to Valentine

EGLAMOUR, agent for Silvia in her escape

SPEED, a clownish servant to Valentine

LAUNCE, the like to Proteus

PANTHINO, servant to Antonio

HOST, where Julia lodges in Milan

OUTLAWS, with Valentine

JULIA, a lady of Verona, beloved of Proteus

SILVIA, beloved of Valentine

LUCETTA, waiting-woman to Julia

SERVANTS, MUSICIANS

SCENE: Verona; Milan; the frontiers of Mantua

ACT 1.

SCENE I. Verona. An open place

[Enter VALENTINE and PROTEUS.]

VALENTINE.

Cease to persuade, my loving Proteus:

Home-keeping youth have ever homely wits.

Were't not affection chains thy tender days

To the sweet glances of thy honour'd love,

I rather would entreat thy company

To see the wonders of the world abroad,

Than, living dully sluggardiz'd at home,

Wear out thy youth with shapeless idleness.

But since thou lov'st, love still, and thrive therein,

Even as I would, when I to love begin.

PROTEUS.

Wilt thou be gone? Sweet Valentine, adieu!

Think on thy Proteus, when thou haply seest

Some rare noteworthy object in thy travel:

Wish me partaker in thy happiness

When thou dost meet good hap; and in thy danger,

If ever danger do environ thee,

Commend thy grievance to my holy prayers,

For I will be thy headsman, Valentine.

VALENTINE.

And on a love-book pray for my success?

PROTEUS.

Upon some book I love I'll pray for thee.

VALENTINE.

That's on some shallow story of deep love,

How young Leander cross'd the Hellespont.

PROTEUS.

That's a deep story of a deeper love;

For he was more than over shoes in love.

VALENTINE.

'Tis true; for you are over boots in love,

And yet you never swum the Hellespont.

PROTEUS.

Over the boots? Nay, give me not the boots.

VALENTINE.

No, I will not, for it boots thee not.

PROTEUS.

What?

VALENTINE.

To be in love, where scorn is bought with groans;

Coy looks with heart-sore sighs; one fading moment's mirth

With twenty watchful, weary, tedious nights:

If haply won, perhaps a hapless gain;

If lost, why then a grievous labour won:

However, but a folly bought with wit,

Or else a wit by folly vanquished.

PROTEUS.

So, by your circumstance, you call me fool.

VALENTINE.

So, by your circumstance, I fear you'll prove.

PROTEUS.

'Tis love you cavil at: I am not Love.

VALENTINE.

Love is your master, for he masters you;

And he that is so yoked by a fool,

Methinks, should not be chronicled for wise.

PROTEUS.

Yet writers say, as in the sweetest bud

The eating canker dwells, so eating love

Inhabits in the finest wits of all.

VALENTINE.

And writers say, as the most forward bud

Is eaten by the canker ere it blow,

Even so by love the young and tender wit

Is turned to folly; blasting in the bud,

Losing his verdure even in the prime,

And all the fair effects of future hopes.

But wherefore waste I time to counsel the

That art a votary to fond desire?

Once more adieu! my father at the road

Expects my coming, there to see me shipp'd.

PROTEUS.

And thither will I bring thee, Valentine.

VALENTINE.

Sweet Proteus, no; now let us take our leave.

To Milan let me hear from thee by letters

Of thy success in love, and what news else

Betideth here in absence of thy friend;

And I likewise will visit thee with mine.

PROTEUS.

All happiness bechance to thee in Milan!

VALENTINE.

As much to you at home! and so farewell!

[Exit.]

PROTEUS.

He after honour hunts, I after love;

He leaves his friends to dignify them more:

I leave myself, my friends, and all for love.

Thou, Julia, thou hast metamorphos'd me;—

Made me neglect my studies, lose my time,

War with good counsel, set the world at nought;

Made wit with musing weak, heart sick with thought.

[Enter SPEED.]

SPEED.

Sir Proteus, save you! Saw you my master?

PROTEUS.

But now he parted hence to embark for Milan.

SPEED.

Twenty to one then he is shipp'd already,

And I have play'd the sheep in losing him.

PROTEUS.

Indeed a sheep doth very often stray,

An if the shepherd be a while away.

SPEED.

You conclude that my master is a shepherd then, and

I a sheep?

PROTEUS.

I do.

SPEED.

Why then, my horns are his horns, whether I wake or sleep.

PROTEUS.

A silly answer, and fitting well a sheep.

SPEED.

This proves me still a sheep.

PROTEUS.

True; and thy master a shepherd.

SPEED.

Nay, that I can deny by a circumstance.

PROTEUS.

It shall go hard but I'll prove it by another.

SPEED. The shepherd seeks the sheep, and not the sheep the shepherd; but I seek my master, and my master seeks not me; therefore, I am no sheep.

PROTEUS. The sheep for fodder follow the shepherd; the shepherd for food follows not the sheep: thou for wages followest thy master; thy master for wages follows not thee. Therefore, thou art a sheep.

SPEED.

Such another proof will make me cry 'baa.'

PROTEUS.

But, dost thou hear? gavest thou my letter to Julia?

SPEED. Ay, sir; I, a lost mutton, gave your letter to her, a laced mutton; and she, a laced mutton, gave me, a lost mutton, nothing for my labour.

PROTEUS.

Here's too small a pasture for such store of muttons.

SPEED.

If the ground be overcharged, you were best stick her.

PROTEUS.

Nay, in that you are astray: 'twere best pound you.

SPEED. Nay, sir, less than a pound shall serve me for carrying your letter.

PROTEUS.

You mistake; I mean the pound,—a pinfold.

SPEED.

From a pound to a pin? fold it over and over,

'Tis threefold too little for carrying a letter to your lover.

PROTEUS.

But what said she? [SPEED nods.] Did she nod?

[SPEED] Ay.

PROTEUS. Nod, ay? Why, that's noddy.

SPEED. You mistook, sir; I say she did nod; and you ask me if she did nod; and I say, Ay.

PROTEUS.

And that set together is—noddy.

SPEED. Now you have taken the pains to set it together, take it for your pains.

PROTEUS.

No, no; you shall have it for bearing the letter.

SPEED.

Well, I perceive I must be fain to bear with you.

PROTEUS.

Why, sir, how do you bear with me?

SPEED. Marry, sir, the letter, very orderly; having nothing but the word 'noddy' for my pains.

PROTEUS.

Beshrew me, but you have a quick wit.

SPEED.

And yet it cannot overtake your slow purse.

PROTEUS.

Come, come; open the matter; in brief: what said she?

SPEED. Open your purse, that the money and the matter may be both at once delivered.

PROTEUS. Well, sir, here is for your pains [giving him money]. What said she?

SPEED.

Truly, sir, I think you'll hardly win her.

PROTEUS.

Why, couldst thou perceive so much from her?

SPEED. Sir, I could perceive nothing at all from her; no, not so much as a ducat for delivering your letter; and being so hard to me that brought your mind, I fear she'll prove as hard to you in telling your mind. Give her no token but stones, for she's as hard as steel.

PROTEUS.

What! said she nothing?

SPEED. No, not so much as 'Take this for thy pains.' To testify your bounty, I thank you, you have testerned me; in requital whereof, henceforth carry your letters yourself; and so, sir, I'll commend you to my master.

PROTEUS.

Go, go, be gone, to save your ship from wrack;

Which cannot perish, having thee aboard,

Being destin'd to a drier death on shore.—

[Exit SPEED.]

I must go send some better messenger.

I fear my Julia would not deign my lines,

Receiving them from such a worthless post.

[Exit.]

SCENE 2. THe same. The garden Of JULIA'S house.

[Enter JULIA and LUCETTA.]

JULIA.

But say, Lucetta, now we are alone,

Wouldst thou then counsel me to fall in love?

LUCETTA.

Ay, madam; so you stumble not unheedfully.

JULIA.

Of all the fair resort of gentlemen

That every day with parle encounter me,

In thy opinion which is worthiest love?

LUCETTA.

Please you, repeat their names; I'll show my mind

According to my shallow simple skill.

JULIA.

What think'st thou of the fair Sir Eglamour?

LUCETTA.

As of a knight well-spoken, neat, and fine;

But, were I you, he never should be mine.

JULIA.

What think'st thou of the rich Mercatio?

LUCETTA.

Well of his wealth; but of himself, so so.

JULIA.

What think'st thou of the gentle Proteus?

LUCETTA.

Lord, Lord! to see what folly reigns in us!

JULIA.

How now! what means this passion at his name?

LUCETTA.

Pardon, dear madam; 'tis a passing shame

That I, unworthy body as I am,

Should censure thus on lovely gentlemen.

JULIA.

Why not on Proteus, as of all the rest?

LUCETTA.

Then thus,—of many good I think him best.

JULIA.

Your reason?

LUCETTA.

I have no other but a woman's reason:

I think him so, because I think him so.

JULIA.

And wouldst thou have me cast my love on him?

LUCETTA.

Ay, if you thought your love not cast away.

JULIA.

Why, he, of all the rest, hath never moved me.

LUCETTA.

Yet he, of all the rest, I think, best loves ye.

JULIA.

His little speaking shows his love but small.

LUCETTA.

Fire that's closest kept burns most of all.

JULIA.

They do not love that do not show their love.

LUCETTA.

O! they love least that let men know their love.

JULIA.

I would I knew his mind.

LUCETTA.

Peruse this paper, madam. [Gives a letter.]

JULIA.

'To Julia'—Say, from whom?

LUCETTA.

That the contents will show.

JULIA.

Say, say, who gave it thee?

LUCETTA.

Sir Valentine's page, and sent, I think, from Proteus.

He would have given it you; but I, being in the way,

Did in your name receive it; pardon the fault, I pray.

JULIA.

Now, by my modesty, a goodly broker!

Dare you presume to harbour wanton lines?

To whisper and conspire against my youth?

Now, trust me, 'tis an office of great worth,

And you an officer fit for the place.

There, take the paper; see it be return'd;

Or else return no more into my sight.

LUCETTA.

To plead for love deserves more fee than hate.

JULIA.

Will ye be gone?

LUCETTA.

That you may ruminate.

[Exit.]

JULIA.

And yet, I would I had o'erlook'd the letter.

It were a shame to call her back again,

And pray her to a fault for which I chid her.

What fool is she, that knows I am a maid

And would not force the letter to my view!

Since maids, in modesty, say 'No' to that

Which they would have the profferer construe 'Ay.'

Fie, fie, how wayward is this foolish love,

That like a testy babe will scratch the nurse,

And presently, all humbled, kiss the rod!

How churlishly I chid Lucetta hence,

When willingly I would have had her here:

How angerly I taught my brow to frown,

When inward joy enforc'd my heart to smile.

My penance is, to call Lucetta back

And ask remission for my folly past.

What ho! Lucetta!

[Re-enter LUCETTA.]

LUCETTA.

What would your ladyship?

JULIA.

Is it near dinner time?

LUCETTA.

I would it were;

That you might kill your stomach on your meat

And not upon your maid.

JULIA.

What is't that you took up so gingerly?

LUCETTA.

Nothing.

JULIA.

Why didst thou stoop, then?

LUCETTA.

To take a paper up

That I let fall.

JULIA.

And is that paper nothing?

LUCETTA.

Nothing concerning me.

JULIA.

Then let it lie for those that it concerns.

LUCETTA.

Madam, it will not lie where it concerns,

Unless it have a false interpreter.

JULIA.

Some love of yours hath writ to you in rime.

LUCETTA.

That I might sing it, madam, to a tune:

Give me a note: your ladyship can set.

JULIA.

As little by such toys as may be possible;

Best sing it to the tune of 'Light o' Love.'

LUCETTA.

It is too heavy for so light a tune.

JULIA.

Heavy! belike it hath some burden then?

LUCETTA.

Ay; and melodious were it, would you sing it.

JULIA.

And why not you?

LUCETTA.

I cannot reach so high.

JULIA.

Let's see your song. [Taking the letter.]

How now, minion!

LUCETTA.

Keep tune there still, so you will sing it out:

And yet methinks, I do not like this tune.

JULIA.

You do not?

LUCETTA.

No, madam; it is too sharp.

JULIA.

You, minion, are too saucy.

LUCETTA.

Nay, now you are too flat

And mar the concord with too harsh a descant;

There wanteth but a mean to fill your song.

JULIA.

The mean is drown'd with your unruly bass.

LUCETTA.

Indeed, I bid the base for Proteus.

JULIA.

This babble shall not henceforth trouble me.

Here is a coil with protestation!—[Tears the letter.]

Go, get you gone; and let the papers lie:

You would be fingering them, to anger me.

LUCETTA.

She makes it strange; but she would be best pleas'd

To be so anger'd with another letter.

[Exit.]

JULIA.

Nay, would I were so anger'd with the same!

O hateful hands, to tear such loving words!

Injurious wasps, to feed on such sweet honey

And kill the bees that yield it with your stings!

I'll kiss each several paper for amends.

Look, here is writ 'kind Julia.' Unkind Julia!

27

As in revenge of thy ingratitude,

I throw thy name against the bruising stones,

Trampling contemptuously on thy disdain.

And here is writ 'love-wounded Proteus':

Poor wounded name! my bosom, as a bed,

Shall lodge thee till thy wound be throughly heal'd;

And thus I search it with a sovereign kiss.

But twice or thrice was 'Proteus' written down:

Be calm, good wind, blow not a word away

Till I have found each letter in the letter

Except mine own name; that some whirlwind bear

Unto a ragged, fearful-hanging rock,

And throw it thence into the raging sea!

Lo, here in one line is his name twice writ:

'Poor forlorn Proteus, passionate Proteus,

To the sweet Julia':—that I'll tear away;

And yet I will not, sith so prettily

He couples it to his complaining names:

Thus will I fold them one upon another:

Now kiss, embrace, contend, do what you will.

[Re-enter LUCETTA.]

LUCETTA.

Madam,

Dinner is ready, and your father stays.

JULIA.

Well, let us go.

LUCETTA.

What! shall these papers lie like tell-tales here?

JULIA.

If you respect them, best to take them up.

LUCETTA.

Nay, I was taken up for laying them down;

Yet here they shall not lie, for catching cold.

JULIA.

I see you have a month's mind to them.

LUCETTA.

Ay, madam, you may say what sights you see;

I see things too, although you judge I wink.

JULIA.

Come, come; will't please you go?

[Exeunt.]

SCENE 3. The same. A room in ANTONIO'S house.

[Enter ANTONIO and PANTHINO.]

ANTONIO.

Tell me, Panthino, what sad talk was that

Wherewith my brother held you in the cloister?

PANTHINO.

'Twas of his nephew Proteus, your son.

ANTONIO.

Why, what of him?

PANTHINO.

He wonder'd that your lordship

Would suffer him to spend his youth at home,

While other men, of slender reputation,

Put forth their sons to seek preferment out:

Some to the wars, to try their fortune there;

Some to discover islands far away;

Some to the studious universities.

For any, or for all these exercises,

He said that Proteus, your son, was meet;

And did request me to importune you

To let him spend his time no more at home,

Which would be great impeachment to his age,

In having known no travel in his youth.

ANTONIO.

Nor need'st thou much importune me to that

Whereon this month I have been hammering.

I have consider'd well his loss of time,

And how he cannot be a perfect man,

Not being tried and tutor'd in the world:

Experience is by industry achiev'd,

And perfected by the swift course of time.

Then tell me whither were I best to send him?

PANTHINO.

I think your lordship is not ignorant

How his companion, youthful Valentine,

Attends the emperor in his royal court.

ANTONIO.

I know it well.

PANTHINO.

'Twere good, I think, your lordship sent him thither:

There shall he practise tilts and tournaments,

Hear sweet discourse, converse with noblemen,

And be in eye of every exercise

Worthy his youth and nobleness of birth.

ANTONIO.

I like thy counsel; well hast thou advis'd;

And that thou mayst perceive how well I like it,

The execution of it shall make known:

Even with the speediest expedition

I will dispatch him to the emperor's court.

PANTHINO.

To-morrow, may it please you, Don Alphonso

With other gentlemen of good esteem

Are journeying to salute the emperor

And to commend their service to his will.

ANTONIO.

Good company; with them shall Proteus go.

And in good time:—now will we break with him.

[Enter PROTEUS.]

PROTEUS.

Sweet love! sweet lines! sweet life!

Here is her hand, the agent of her heart;

Here is her oath for love, her honour's pawn.

O! that our fathers would applaud our loves,

To seal our happiness with their consents!

O heavenly Julia!

ANTONIO.

How now! What letter are you reading there?

PROTEUS.

May't please your lordship, 'tis a word or two

Of commendations sent from Valentine,

Deliver'd by a friend that came from him.

ANTONIO.

Lend me the letter; let me see what news.

PROTEUS.

There is no news, my lord; but that he writes

How happily he lives, how well belov'd

And daily graced by the emperor;

Wishing me with him, partner of his fortune.

ANTONIO.

And how stand you affected to his wish?

PROTEUS.

As one relying on your lordship's will,

And not depending on his friendly wish.

ANTONIO.

My will is something sorted with his wish.

Muse not that I thus suddenly proceed;

For what I will, I will, and there an end.

I am resolv'd that thou shalt spend some time

With Valentinus in the Emperor's court:

What maintenance he from his friends receives,

Like exhibition thou shalt have from me.

To-morrow be in readiness to go:

Excuse it not, for I am peremptory.

PROTEUS.

My lord, I cannot be so soon provided;

Please you, deliberate a day or two.

ANTONIO.

Look, what thou want'st shall be sent after thee:

No more of stay; to-morrow thou must go.

Come on, Panthino: you shall be employ'd

To hasten on his expedition.

[Exeunt ANTONIO and PANTHINO.]

PROTEUS.

Thus have I shunn'd the fire for fear of burning,

And drench'd me in the sea, where I am drown'd.

I fear'd to show my father Julia's letter,

Lest he should take exceptions to my love;

And with the vantage of mine own excuse

Hath he excepted most against my love.

O! how this spring of love resembleth

The uncertain glory of an April day,

Which now shows all the beauty of the sun,

And by an by a cloud takes all away!

[Re-enter PANTHINO.]

PANTHINO.

Sir Proteus, your father calls for you;

He is in haste; therefore, I pray you, go.

PROTEUS.

Why, this it is: my heart accords thereto,

And yet a thousand times it answers 'no.'

[Exeunt.]

ACT 2.

SCENE I. Milan. A room in the DUKE'S palace.

[Enter VALENTINE and SPEED.]

SPEED.

Sir, your glove. [Offering a glove.]

VALENTINE.

Not mine; my gloves are on.

SPEED.

Why, then, this may be yours; for this is but one.

VALENTINE.

Ha! let me see; ay, give it me, it's mine;

Sweet ornament that decks a thing divine!

Ah, Silvia! Silvia!

SPEED.

[Calling.] Madam Silvia! Madam Silvia!

VALENTINE.

How now, sirrah?

SPEED.

She is not within hearing, sir.

VALENTINE.

Why, sir, who bade you call her?

SPEED.

Your worship, sir; or else I mistook.

VALENTINE.

Well, you'll still be too forward.

SPEED.

And yet I was last chidden for being too slow.

VALENTINE.

Go to, sir. tell me, do you know Madam Silvia?

SPEED.

She that your worship loves?

VALENTINE.

Why, how know you that I am in love?

SPEED. Marry, by these special marks: first, you have learned, like Sir Proteus, to wreath your arms like a malcontent; to relish a love-song, like a robin redbreast; to walk alone, like one that had the pestilence; to sigh, like a school-boy that had lost his A B C; to weep, like a young wench that had buried her grandam; to fast, like one that takes diet; to watch, like one that fears robbing; to speak puling, like a beggar at Hallowmas. You were wont, when you laughed, to crow like a cock; when you walked, to walk like one of the lions; when you fasted, it was presently after dinner; when you looked sadly, it was for want of money. And now you are metamorphosed with a mistress, that, when I look on you, I can hardly think you my master.

VALENTINE.

Are all these things perceived in me?

SPEED.

They are all perceived without ye.

VALENTINE.

Without me? They cannot.

SPEED. Without you? Nay, that's certain; for, without you were so simple, none else would; but you are so without these follies that these follies are within you, and shine through you like the water in an urinal, that not an eye that sees you but is a physician to comment on your malady.

VALENTINE.

But tell me, dost thou know my lady Silvia?

SPEED.

She that you gaze on so as she sits at supper?

VALENTINE.

Hast thou observed that? Even she, I mean.

SPEED.

Why, sir, I know her not.

VALENTINE. Dost thou know her by my gazing on her, and yet know'st her not?

SPEED.

Is she not hard-favoured, sir?

VALENTINE.

Not so fair, boy, as well-favoured.

SPEED.

Sir, I know that well enough.

VALENTINE.

What dost thou know?

SPEED.

That she is not so fair as, of you, well-favoured.

VALENTINE. I mean that her beauty is exquisite, but her favour infinite.

SPEED. That's because the one is painted, and the other out of all count.

VALENTINE.

How painted? and how out of count?

SPEED. Marry, sir, so painted to make her fair, that no man counts of her beauty.

VALENTINE.

How esteem'st thou me? I account of her beauty.

SPEED.

You never saw her since she was deformed.

VALENTINE.

How long hath she been deformed?

SPEED.

Ever since you loved her.

VALENTINE.

I have loved her ever since I saw her, and still

I see her beautiful.

SPEED.

If you love her, you cannot see her.

VALENTINE.

Why?

SPEED.

Because Love is blind. O! that you had mine eyes; or your own

eyes had the lights they were wont to have when you chid at Sir

Proteus for going ungartered!

VALENTINE.

What should I see then?

SPEED. Your own present folly and her passing deformity; for he, being in love, could not see to garter his hose; and you, being in love, cannot see to put on your hose.

VALENTINE. Belike, boy, then you are in love; for last morning you could not see to wipe my shoes.

SPEED. True, sir; I was in love with my bed. I thank you, you swinged me for my love, which makes me the bolder to chide you for yours.

VALENTINE.

In conclusion, I stand affected to her.

SPEED.

I would you were set, so your affection would cease.

VALENTINE. Last night she enjoined me to write some lines to one she loves.

SPEED.

And have you?

VALENTINE.

I have.

SPEED.

Are they not lamely writ?

VALENTINE.

No, boy, but as well as I can do them.

Peace! here she comes.

[Enter SILVIA.]

SPEED.

[Aside] O excellent motion! O exceeding puppet!

Now will he interpret to her.

VALENTINE.

Madam and mistress, a thousand good morrows.

SPEED.

[Aside] O, give ye good even: here's a million of manners.

SILVIA.

Sir Valentine and servant, to you two thousand.

SPEED. [Aside] He should give her interest, and she gives it him.

VALENTINE.

As you enjoin'd me, I have writ your letter

Unto the secret nameless friend of yours;

Which I was much unwilling to proceed in,

But for my duty to your ladyship.

[Gives a letter.]

SILVIA.

I thank you, gentle servant. 'Tis very clerkly done.

VALENTINE.

Now trust me, madam, it came hardly off;

For, being ignorant to whom it goes,

I writ at random, very doubtfully.

SILVIA.

Perchance you think too much of so much pains?

VALENTINE.

No, madam; so it stead you, I will write,

Please you command, a thousand times as much;

And yet—

SILVIA.

A pretty period! Well, I guess the sequel;

And yet I will not name it; and yet I care not.

And yet take this again; and yet I thank you,

Meaning henceforth to trouble you no more.

SPEED.

[Aside] And yet you will; and yet another yet.

VALENTINE.

What means your ladyship? Do you not like it?

SILVIA.

Yes, yes; the lines are very quaintly writ;

But, since unwillingly, take them again:

Nay, take them.

[Gives hack the letter.]

VALENTINE.

Madam, they are for you.

SILVIA.

Ay, ay, you writ them, sir, at my request;

But I will none of them; they are for you.

I would have had them writ more movingly.

VALENTINE.

Please you, I'll write your ladyship another.

SILVIA.

And when it's writ, for my sake read it over;

And if it please you, so; if not, why, so.

VALENTINE.

If it please me, madam, what then?

SILVIA.

Why, if it please you, take it for your labour.

And so good morrow, servant.

[Exit.]

SPEED.

O jest unseen, inscrutable, invisible,

As a nose on a man's face, or a weathercock on a steeple!

My master sues to her; and she hath taught her suitor,

He being her pupil, to become her tutor.

O excellent device! Was there ever heard a better,

That my master, being scribe, to himself should write the letter?

VALENTINE.

How now, sir! What are you reasoning with yourself?

SPEED.

Nay, I was rhyming: 'tis you that have the reason.

VALENTINE.

To do what?

SPEED.

To be a spokesman from Madam Silvia.

VALENTINE.

To whom?

SPEED.

To yourself; why, she woos you by a figure.

VALENTINE.

What figure?

SPEED.

By a letter, I should say.

VALENTINE.

Why, she hath not writ to me?

SPEED.

What need she, when she hath made you write to yourself?

Why, do you not perceive the jest?

VALENTINE.

No, believe me.

SPEED. No believing you indeed, sir. But did you perceive her earnest?

VALENTINE.

She gave me none except an angry word.

SPEED.

Why, she hath given you a letter.

VALENTINE.

That's the letter I writ to her friend.

SPEED.

And that letter hath she delivered, and there an end.

VALENTINE.

I would it were no worse.

SPEED.

I'll warrant you 'tis as well.

'For often have you writ to her; and she, in modesty,

Or else for want of idle time, could not again reply;

Or fearing else some messenger that might her mind discover,

Herself hath taught her love himself to write unto her lover.'

All this I speak in print, for in print I found it.

Why muse you, sir? 'Tis dinner time.

VALENTINE.

I have dined.

SPEED. Ay, but hearken, sir; though the chameleon Love can feed on the air, I am one that am nourished by my victuals, and would fain have meat. O! be not like your mistress! Be moved, be moved.

[Exeunt.]

SCENE 2. Verona. A room in JULIA'S house.

[Enter PROTEUS and JULIA.]

PROTEUS.

Have patience, gentle Julia.

JULIA.

I must, where is no remedy.

PROTEUS.

When possibly I can, I will return.

JULIA.

If you turn not, you will return the sooner.

Keep this remembrance for thy Julia's sake.

[Gives him a ring.]

PROTEUS.

Why, then, we'll make exchange. Here, take you this.

[Gives her another.]

JULIA.

And seal the bargain with a holy kiss.

PROTEUS.

Here is my hand for my true constancy;

And when that hour o'erslips me in the day

Wherein I sigh not, Julia, for thy sake,

The next ensuing hour some foul mischance

Torment me for my love's forgetfulness!

My father stays my coming; answer not;

The tide is now: nay, not thy tide of tears:

That tide will stay me longer than I should.

Julia, farewell!

[Exit JULIA.]

What, gone without a word?

Ay, so true love should do: it cannot speak;

For truth hath better deeds than words to grace it.

[Enter PANTHINO.]

PANTHINO.

Sir Proteus, you are stay'd for.

PROTEUS.

Go; I come, I come.

Alas! this parting strikes poor lovers dumb.

[Exeunt.]

SCENE 3. The same. A street

[Enter LAUNCE, leading a dog.]

LAUNCE. Nay, 'twill be this hour ere I have done weeping; all the kind of the Launces have this very fault. I have received my proportion, like the prodigious son, and am going with Sir Proteus to the imperial's court. I think Crab my dog be the sourest-natured dog that lives: my mother weeping, my father wailing, my sister crying, our maid howling, our cat wringing her hands, and all our house in a great perplexity; yet did not this cruel-hearted cur shed one tear. He is a stone, a very pebble stone, and has no more pity in him than a dog; a Jew would have wept to have seen our parting; why, my grandam having no eyes, look you, wept herself blind at my parting. Nay, I'll show you the manner of it. This shoe is my father; no, this left shoe is my father; no, no, left shoe is my mother; nay, that cannot be so neither; yes, it is so, it is so, it hath the worser sole. This shoe with the hole in it is my mother, and this my father. A vengeance on 't! There 'tis: now, sir, this staff is my sister, for, look you, she is as white as a lily and as small as a wand; this hat is Nan our maid; I am the dog; no, the dog is himself, and I am the dog—O! the dog is me, and I am myself; ay, so, so. Now come I to my father: 'Father, your blessing.' Now should not the shoe speak a word for weeping; now should I kiss my father; well, he weeps on. Now come I to my mother;—O, that she could speak now like a wood woman! Well, I kiss her; why there 'tis; here's my mother's breath up and down. Now come I to my sister; mark the moan she makes. Now the dog all this while sheds not a tear, nor speaks a word; but see how I lay the dust with my tears.

[Enter PANTHINO.]

PANTHINO. Launce, away, away, aboard! Thy master is shipped, and thou art to post after with oars. What's the matter? Why weep'st thou, man? Away, ass! You'll lose the tide if you tarry any longer.

LAUNCE. It is no matter if the tied were lost; for it is the unkindest tied that ever any man tied.

PANTHINO.

What's the unkindest tide?

LAUNCE.

Why, he that's tied here, Crab, my dog.

PANTHINO. Tut, man, I mean thou'lt lose the flood, and, in losing the flood, lose thy voyage, and, in losing thy voyage, lose thy master, and, in losing thy master, lose thy service, and, in losing thy service,—Why dost thou stop my mouth?

LAUNCE.

For fear thou shouldst lose thy tongue.

PANTHINO.

Where should I lose my tongue?

LAUNCE.

In thy tale.

PANTHINO.

In thy tail!

LAUNCE. Lose the tide, and the voyage, and the master, and the service, and the tied! Why, man, if the river were dry, I am able to fill it with my tears; if the wind were down, I could drive the boat with my sighs.

PANTHINO.

Come, come away, man; I was sent to call thee.

LAUNCE.

Sir, call me what thou darest.

PANTHINO.

Will thou go?

LAUNCE.

Well, I will go.

[Exeunt.]

SCENE 4. Milan. A room in the DUKE'S palace.

[Enter SILVIA, VALENTINE, THURIO, and SPEED.]

SILVIA.

Servant!

VALENTINE.

Mistress?

SPEED.

Master, Sir Thurio frowns on you.

VALENTINE.

Ay, boy, it's for love.

SPEED.

Not of you.

VALENTINE.

Of my mistress, then.

SPEED.

'Twere good you knock'd him.

SILVIA.

Servant, you are sad.

VALENTINE.

Indeed, madam, I seem so.

THURIO.

Seem you that you are not?

VALENTINE.

Haply I do.

THURIO.

So do counterfeits.

VALENTINE.

So do you.

THURIO.

What seem I that I am not?

VALENTINE.

Wise.

THURIO.

What instance of the contrary?

VALENTINE.

Your folly.

THURIO.

And how quote you my folly?

VALENTINE.

I quote it in your jerkin.

THURIO.

My jerkin is a doublet.

VALENTINE.

Well, then, I'll double your folly.

THURIO.

How?

SILVIA.

What, angry, Sir Thurio! Do you change colour?

VALENTINE.

Give him leave, madam; he is a kind of chameleon.

THURIO. That hath more mind to feed on your blood than live in your air.

VALENTINE.

You have said, sir.

THURIO.

Ay, sir, and done too, for this time.

VALENTINE.

I know it well, sir; you always end ere you begin.

SILVIA.

A fine volley of words, gentlemen, and quickly shot off.

VALENTINE.

'Tis indeed, madam; we thank the giver.

SILVIA.

Who is that, servant?

VALENTINE. Yourself, sweet lady; for you gave the fire. Sir Thurio borrows his wit from your ladyship's looks, and spends what he borrows kindly in your company.

THURIO. Sir, if you spend word for word with me, I shall make your wit bankrupt.

VALENTINE. I know it well, sir; you have an exchequer of words, and,

I think, no other treasure to give your followers; for it appears by their bare liveries that they live by your bare words.

[Enter DUKE]

SILVIA.

No more, gentlemen, no more. Here comes my father.

[Enter DUKE.]

DUKE.

Now, daughter Silvia, you are hard beset.

Sir Valentine, your father is in good health.

What say you to a letter from your friends

Of much good news?

VALENTINE.

My lord, I will be thankful

To any happy messenger from thence.

DUKE.

Know ye Don Antonio, your countryman?

VALENTINE.

Ay, my good lord, I know the gentleman

To be of worth and worthy estimation,

And not without desert so well reputed.

DUKE.

Hath he not a son?

VALENTINE.

Ay, my good lord; a son that well deserves

The honour and regard of such a father.

DUKE.

You know him well?

VALENTINE.

I knew him as myself; for from our infancy

We have convers'd and spent our hours together;

And though myself have been an idle truant,

Omitting the sweet benefit of time

To clothe mine age with angel-like perfection,

Yet hath Sir Proteus,—for that's his name,—

Made use and fair advantage of his days:

His years but young, but his experience old;

His head unmellowed, but his judgment ripe;

And, in a word,—for far behind his worth

Comes all the praises that I now bestow,—

He is complete in feature and in mind,

With all good grace to grace a gentleman.

DUKE.

Beshrew me, sir, but if he make this good,

He is as worthy for an empress' love

As meet to be an emperor's counsellor.

Well, sir, this gentleman is come to me

With commendation from great potentates,

And here he means to spend his time awhile.

I think 'tis no unwelcome news to you.

VALENTINE.

Should I have wish'd a thing, it had been he.

DUKE.

Welcome him, then, according to his worth.

Silvia, I speak to you, and you, Sir Thurio:—

For Valentine, I need not cite him to it.

I will send him hither to you presently.

[Exit.]

VALENTINE.

This is the gentleman I told your ladyship

Had come along with me but that his mistresss

Did hold his eyes lock'd in her crystal looks.

SILVIA.

Belike that now she hath enfranchis'd them

Upon some other pawn for fealty.

VALENTINE.

Nay, sure, I think she holds them prisoners still.

SILVIA.

Nay, then, he should be blind; and, being blind,

How could he see his way to seek out you?

VALENTINE.

Why, lady, Love hath twenty pair of eyes.

THURIO.

They say that Love hath not an eye at all.

VALENTINE.

To see such lovers, Thurio, as yourself:

Upon a homely object Love can wink.

SILVIA.

Have done, have done; here comes the gentleman.

[Enter PROTEUS]

VALENTINE.

Welcome, dear Proteus! Mistress, I beseech you

Confirm his welcome with some special favour.

SILVIA.

His worth is warrant for his welcome hither,

If this be he you oft have wish'd to hear from.

VALENTINE.

Mistress, it is; sweet lady, entertain him

To be my fellow-servant to your ladyship.

SILVIA.

Too low a mistress for so high a servant.

PROTEUS.

Not so, sweet lady; but too mean a servant

To have a look of such a worthy mistress.

VALENTINE.

Leave off discourse of disability;

Sweet lady, entertain him for your servant.

PROTEUS.

My duty will I boast of, nothing else.

SILVIA.

And duty never yet did want his meed.

Servant, you are welcome to a worthless mistress.

PROTEUS.

I'll die on him that says so but yourself.

SILVIA.

That you are welcome?

PROTEUS.

That you are worthless.

[Enter a servant.]

SERVANT.

Madam, my lord your father would speak with you.

SILVIA.

I wait upon his pleasure.

[Exit Servant.]

Come, Sir Thurio,

Go with me. Once more, new servant, welcome.

I'll leave you to confer of home affairs;

When you have done we look to hear from you.

PROTEUS.

We'll both attend upon your ladyship.

[Exeunt SILVIA, THURIO, and SPEED.]

VALENTINE.

Now, tell me, how do all from whence you came?

PROTEUS.

Your friends are well, and have them much commended.

VALENTINE.

And how do yours?

PROTEUS.

I left them all in health.

VALENTINE.

How does your lady, and how thrives your love?

PROTEUS.

My tales of love were wont to weary you;

I know you joy not in a love-discourse.

VALENTINE.

Ay, Proteus, but that life is alter'd now;

I have done penance for contemning Love;

Whose high imperious thoughts have punish'd me

With bitter fasts, with penitential groans,

With nightly tears, and daily heart-sore sighs;

For, in revenge of my contempt of love,

Love hath chas'd sleep from my enthralled eyes

And made them watchers of mine own heart's sorrow.

O, gentle Proteus! Love's a mighty lord,

And hath so humbled me as I confess,

There is no woe to his correction,

Nor to his service no such joy on earth.

Now no discourse, except it be of love;

Now can I break my fast, dine, sup, and sleep,

Upon the very naked name of love.

PROTEUS.

Enough; I read your fortune in your eye.

Was this the idol that you worship so?

VALENTINE.

Even she; and is she not a heavenly saint?

PROTEUS.

No; but she is an earthly paragon.

VALENTINE.

Call her divine.

PROTEUS.

I will not flatter her.

VALENTINE.

O! flatter me; for love delights in praises.

PROTEUS.

When I was sick you gave me bitter pills,

And I must minister the like to you.

VALENTINE.

Then speak the truth by her; if not divine,

Yet let her be a principality,

Sovereign to all the creatures on the earth.

PROTEUS.

Except my mistress.

VALENTINE.

Sweet, except not any,

Except thou wilt except against my love.

PROTEUS.

Have I not reason to prefer mine own?

VALENTINE.

And I will help thee to prefer her too:

She shall be dignified with this high honour,—

To bear my lady's train, lest the base earth

Should from her vesture chance to steal a kiss,

And, of so great a favour growing proud,

Disdain to root the summer-swelling flower

And make rough winter everlastingly.

PROTEUS.

Why, Valentine, what braggardism is this?

VALENTINE.

Pardon me, Proteus; all I can is nothing

To her, whose worth makes other worthies nothing;

She is alone.

PROTEUS.

Then, let her alone.

VALENTINE.

Not for the world: why, man, she is mine own;

And I as rich in having such a jewel

As twenty seas, if all their sand were pearl,

The water nectar, and the rocks pure gold.

Forgive me that I do not dream on thee,

Because thou see'st me dote upon my love.

My foolish rival, that her father likes

Only for his possessions are so huge,

Is gone with her along; and I must after,

For love, thou know'st, is full of jealousy.

PROTEUS.

But she loves you?

VALENTINE.

Ay, and we are betroth'd; nay more, our marriage-hour,

With all the cunning manner of our flight,

Determin'd of: how I must climb her window,

The ladder made of cords, and all the means

Plotted and 'greed on for my happiness.

Good Proteus, go with me to my chamber,

In these affairs to aid me with thy counsel.

PROTEUS.

Go on before; I shall enquire you forth:

I must unto the road to disembark

Some necessaries that I needs must use;

And then I'll presently attend you.

VALENTINE.

Will you make haste?

PROTEUS.

I will.

[Exit VALENTINE.]

Even as one heat another heat expels

Or as one nail by strength drives out another,

So the remembrance of my former love

Is by a newer object quite forgotten.

Is it my mind, or Valentinus' praise,

Her true perfection, or my false transgression,

That makes me reasonless to reason thus?

She is fair; and so is Julia that I love,—

That I did love, for now my love is thaw'd;

Which like a waxen image 'gainst a fire

Bears no impression of the thing it was.

Methinks my zeal to Valentine is cold,

And that I love him not as I was wont.

O! but I love his lady too-too much,

And that's the reason I love him so little.

How shall I dote on her with more advice

That thus without advice begin to love her?

'Tis but her picture I have yet beheld,

And that hath dazzled my reason's light;

But when I look on her perfections,

There is no reason but I shall be blind.

If I can check my erring love, I will;

If not, to compass her I'll use my skill.

[Exit.]

SCENE 5. The same. A street

[Enter SPEED and LAUNCE.]

SPEED.

Launce! by mine honesty, welcome to Milan!

LAUNCE. Forswear not thyself, sweet youth, for I am not welcome. I reckon this always, that a man is never undone till he be hanged, nor never welcome to a place till some certain shot be paid, and the hostess say 'Welcome!'

SPEED. Come on, you madcap; I'll to the alehouse with you presently; where, for one shot of five pence, thou shalt have five thousand welcomes. But, sirrah, how did thy master part with Madam Julia?

LAUNCE. Marry, after they clos'd in earnest, they parted very fairly in jest.

SPEED.

But shall she marry him?

LAUNCE.

No.

SPEED.

How then? Shall he marry her?

LAUNCE.

No, neither.

SPEED.

What, are they broken?

LAUNCE.

No, they are both as whole as a fish.

SPEED.

Why then, how stands the matter with them?

LAUNCE. Marry, thus: when it stands well with him, it stands well with her.

SPEED.

What an ass art thou! I understand thee not.

LAUNCE. What a block art thou that thou canst not! My staff understands me.

SPEED.

What thou sayest?

LAUNCE. Ay, and what I do too; look thee, I'll but lean, and my staff understands me.

SPEED.

It stands under thee, indeed.

LAUNCE.

Why, stand-under and under-stand is all one.

SPEED.

But tell me true, will't be a match?

LAUNCE. Ask my dog. If he say ay, it will; if he say no, it will; if he shake his tail and say nothing, it will.

SPEED.

The conclusion is, then, that it will.

LAUNCE. Thou shalt never get such a secret from me but by a parable.

SPEED. 'Tis well that I get it so. But, Launce, how sayest thou that my master is become a notable lover?

LAUNCE.

I never knew him otherwise.

SPEED.

Than how?

LAUNCE.

A notable lubber, as thou reportest him to be.

SPEED.

Why, thou whoreson ass, thou mistak'st me.

LAUNCE.

Why, fool, I meant not thee, I meant thy master.

SPEED.

I tell thee my master is become a hot lover.

LAUNCE.

Why, I tell thee I care not though he burn himself in love.

If thou wilt, go with me to the alehouse; if not, thou art an

Hebrew, a Jew, and not worth the name of a Christian.

SPEED.

Why?

LAUNCE. Because thou hast not so much charity in thee as to go to the
ale with a Christian. Wilt thou go?

SPEED.

At thy service.

[Exeunt.]

SCENE 6. The same. The DUKE's palace.

[Enter PROTEUS.]

PROTEUS.

To leave my Julia, shall I be forsworn;

To love fair Silvia, shall I be forsworn;

To wrong my friend, I shall be much forsworn;

And even that power which gave me first my oath

Provokes me to this threefold perjury:

Love bade me swear, and Love bids me forswear.

O sweet-suggesting Love! if thou hast sinn'd,

Teach me, thy tempted subject, to excuse it.

At first I did adore a twinkling star,

But now I worship a celestial sun.

Unheedful vows may heedfully be broken;

And he wants wit that wants resolved will

To learn his wit t' exchange the bad for better.

Fie, fie, unreverend tongue, to call her bad,

Whose sovereignty so oft thou hast preferr'd

With twenty thousand soul-confirming oaths.

I cannot leave to love, and yet I do;

But there I leave to love where I should love.

Julia I lose, and Valentine I lose;

If I keep them, I needs must lose myself;

If I lose them, thus find I by their loss,

For Valentine, myself; for Julia, Silvia.

I to myself am dearer than a friend,

For love is still most precious in itself;

And Silvia—witness heaven, that made her fair!—

Shows Julia but a swarthy Ethiope.

I will forget that Julia is alive,

Remembering that my love to her is dead;

And Valentine I'll hold an enemy,

Aiming at Silvia as a sweeter friend.

I cannot now prove constant to myself

Without some treachery us'd to Valentine.

This night he meaneth with a corded ladder

To climb celestial Silvia's chamber window,

Myself in counsel, his competitor.

Now presently I'll give her father notice

Of their disguising and pretended flight;

Who, all enrag'd, will banish Valentine;

For Thurio, he intends, shall wed his daughter;

But, Valentine being gone, I'll quickly cross,

By some sly trick blunt Thurio's dull proceeding.

Love, lend me wings to make my purpose swift,

As thou hast lent me wit to plot this drift!

[Exit.]

SCENE 7. Verona. A room in JULIA'S house.

[Enter JULIA and LUCETTA.]

JULIA.

Counsel, Lucetta; gentle girl, assist me:

And, ev'n in kind love, I do conjure thee,

Who art the table wherein all my thoughts

Are visibly character'd and engrav'd,

To lesson me and tell me some good mean

How, with my honour, I may undertake

A journey to my loving Proteus.

LUCETTA.

Alas, the way is wearisome and long.

JULIA.

A true-devoted pilgrim is not weary

To measure kingdoms with his feeble steps;

Much less shall she that hath Love's wings to fly,

And when the flight is made to one so dear,

Of such divine perfection, as Sir Proteus.

LUCETTA.

Better forbear till Proteus make return.

JULIA.

O! know'st thou not his looks are my soul's food?

Pity the dearth that I have pined in

By longing for that food so long a time.

Didst thou but know the inly touch of love.

Thou wouldst as soon go kindle fire with snow

As seek to quench the fire of love with words.

LUCETTA.

I do not seek to quench your love's hot fire,

But qualify the fire's extreme rage,

Lest it should burn above the bounds of reason.

JULIA.

The more thou damm'st it up, the more it burns.

The current that with gentle murmur glides,

Thou know'st, being stopp'd, impatiently doth rage;

But when his fair course is not hindered,

He makes sweet music with th' enamell'd stones,

Giving a gentle kiss to every sedge

He overtaketh in his pilgrimage;

And so by many winding nooks he strays,

With willing sport, to the wild ocean.

Then let me go, and hinder not my course.

I'll be as patient as a gentle stream,

And make a pastime of each weary step,

Till the last step have brought me to my love;

And there I'll rest as, after much turmoil,

A blessed soul doth in Elysium.

LUCETTA.

But in what habit will you go along?

JULIA.

Not like a woman, for I would prevent

The loose encounters of lascivious men.

Gentle Lucetta, fit me with such weeds

As may beseem some well-reputed page.

LUCETTA.

Why then, your ladyship must cut your hair.

JULIA.

No, girl; I'll knit it up in silken strings

With twenty odd-conceited true-love knots:

To be fantastic may become a youth

Of greater time than I shall show to be.

LUCETTA.

What fashion, madam, shall I make your breeches?

JULIA.

That fits as well as 'Tell me, good my lord,

What compass will you wear your farthingale?'

Why even what fashion thou best likes, Lucetta.

LUCETTA.

You must needs have them with a codpiece, madam.

JULIA.

Out, out, Lucetta, that will be ill-favour'd.

LUCETTA.

A round hose, madam, now's not worth a pin,

Unless you have a codpiece to stick pins on.

JULIA.

Lucetta, as thou lov'st me, let me have

What thou think'st meet, and is most mannerly.

But tell me, wench, how will the world repute me

For undertaking so unstaid a journey?

I fear me it will make me scandaliz'd.

LUCETTA.

If you think so, then stay at home and go not.

JULIA.

Nay, that I will not.

LUCETTA.

Then never dream on infamy, but go.

If Proteus like your journey when you come,

No matter who's displeas'd when you are gone.

I fear me he will scarce be pleas'd withal.

JULIA.

That is the least, Lucetta, of my fear:

A thousand oaths, an ocean of his tears,

And instances of infinite of love,

Warrant me welcome to my Proteus.

LUCETTA.

All these are servants to deceitful men.

JULIA.

Base men that use them to so base effect!

But truer stars did govern Proteus' birth;

His words are bonds, his oaths are oracles,

His love sincere, his thoughts immaculate,

His tears pure messengers sent from his heart,

His heart as far from fraud as heaven from earth.

LUCETTA.

Pray heav'n he prove so when you come to him.

JULIA.

Now, as thou lov'st me, do him not that wrong

To bear a hard opinion of his truth;

Only deserve my love by loving him.

And presently go with me to my chamber,

To take a note of what I stand in need of

To furnish me upon my longing journey.

All that is mine I leave at thy dispose,

My goods, my lands, my reputation;

Only, in lieu thereof, dispatch me hence.

Come, answer not, but to it presently!

I am impatient of my tarriance.

[Exeunt.]

ACT 3.

SCENE I. Milan. An anteroom in the DUKE'S palace.

[Enter DUKE, THURIO, and PROTEUS.]

DUKE.

Sir Thurio, give us leave, I pray, awhile;

We have some secrets to confer about.

[Exit THURIO.]

Now tell me, Proteus, what's your will with me?

PROTEUS.

My gracious lord, that which I would discover

The law of friendship bids me to conceal;

But, when I call to mind your gracious favours

Done to me, undeserving as I am,

My duty pricks me on to utter that

Which else no worldly good should draw from me.

Know, worthy prince, Sir Valentine, my friend,

This night intends to steal away your daughter;

Myself am one made privy to the plot.

I know you have determin'd to bestow her

On Thurio, whom your gentle daughter hates;

And should she thus be stol'n away from you,

It would be much vexation to your age.

Thus, for my duty's sake, I rather chose

To cross my friend in his intended drift

Than, by concealing it, heap on your head

A pack of sorrows which would press you down,

Being unprevented, to your timeless grave.

DUKE.

Proteus, I thank thee for thine honest care,

Which to requite, command me while I live.

This love of theirs myself have often seen,

Haply when they have judg'd me fast asleep,

And oftentimes have purpos'd to forbid

Sir Valentine her company and my court;

But, fearing lest my jealous aim might err

And so, unworthily, disgrace the man,—

A rashness that I ever yet have shunn'd,—

I gave him gentle looks, thereby to find

That which thyself hast now disclos'd to me.

And, that thou mayst perceive my fear of this,

Knowing that tender youth is soon suggested,

I nightly lodge her in an upper tower,

The key whereof myself have ever kept;

And thence she cannot be convey'd away.

PROTEUS.

Know, noble lord, they have devis'd a mean

How he her chamber window will ascend

And with a corded ladder fetch her down;

For which the youthful lover now is gone,

And this way comes he with it presently;

Where, if it please you, you may intercept him.

But, good my lord, do it so cunningly

That my discovery be not aimed at;

For love of you, not hate unto my friend,

Hath made me publisher of this pretence.

DUKE.

Upon mine honour, he shall never know

That I had any light from thee of this.

PROTEUS.

Adieu, my lord; Sir Valentine is coming.

[Exit.]

[Enter VALENTINE]

DUKE.

Sir Valentine, whither away so fast?

VALENTINE.

Please it your Grace, there is a messenger

That stays to bear my letters to my friends,

And I am going to deliver them.

DUKE.

Be they of much import?

VALENTINE.

The tenour of them doth but signify

My health and happy being at your court.

DUKE.

Nay then, no matter; stay with me awhile;

I am to break with thee of some affairs

That touch me near, wherein thou must be secret.

'Tis not unknown to thee that I have sought

To match my friend Sir Thurio to my daughter.

VALENTINE.

I know it well, my lord; and, sure, the match

Were rich and honourable; besides, the gentleman

Is full of virtue, bounty, worth, and qualities

Beseeming such a wife as your fair daughter.

Cannot your grace win her to fancy him?

DUKE.

No, trust me; she is peevish, sullen, froward,

Proud, disobedient, stubborn, lacking duty;

Neither regarding that she is my child

Nor fearing me as if I were her father;

And, may I say to thee, this pride of hers,

Upon advice, hath drawn my love from her;

And, where I thought the remnant of mine age

Should have been cherish'd by her childlike duty,

I now am full resolv'd to take a wife

And turn her out to who will take her in.

Then let her beauty be her wedding-dower;

For me and my possessions she esteems not.

VALENTINE.

What would your Grace have me to do in this?

DUKE.

There is a lady of Verona here,

Whom I affect; but she is nice, and coy,

And nought esteems my aged eloquence.

Now, therefore, would I have thee to my tutor,

For long agone I have forgot to court;

Besides, the fashion of the time is chang'd,

How and which way I may bestow myself

To be regarded in her sun-bright eye.

VALENTINE.

Win her with gifts, if she respect not words:

Dumb jewels often in their silent kind

More than quick words do move a woman's mind.

DUKE.

But she did scorn a present that I sent her.

VALENTINE.

A woman sometime scorns what best contents her.

Send her another; never give her o'er,

For scorn at first makes after-love the more.

If she do frown, 'tis not in hate of you,

But rather to beget more love in you;

If she do chide, 'tis not to have you gone;

For why, the fools are mad if left alone.

Take no repulse, whatever she doth say;

For 'Get you gone' she doth not mean 'Away!'

Flatter and praise, commend, extol their graces;

Though ne'er so black, say they have angels' faces.

That man that hath a tongue, I say, is no man,

If with his tongue he cannot win a woman.

DUKE.

But she I mean is promis'd by her friends

Unto a youthful gentleman of worth;

And kept severely from resort of men,

That no man hath access by day to her.

VALENTINE.

Why then I would resort to her by night.

DUKE.

Ay, but the doors be lock'd and keys kept safe,

That no man hath recourse to her by night.

VALENTINE.

What lets but one may enter at her window?

DUKE.

Her chamber is aloft, far from the ground,

And built so shelving that one cannot climb it

Without apparent hazard of his life.

VALENTINE.

Why then a ladder, quaintly made of cords,

To cast up with a pair of anchoring hooks,

Would serve to scale another Hero's tow'r,

So bold Leander would adventure it.

DUKE.

Now, as thou art a gentleman of blood,

Advise me where I may have such a ladder.

VALENTINE.

When would you use it? Pray, sir, tell me that.

DUKE.

This very night; for Love is like a child,

That longs for everything that he can come by.

VALENTINE.

By seven o'clock I'll get you such a ladder.

DUKE.

But, hark thee; I will go to her alone;

How shall I best convey the ladder thither?

VALENTINE.

It will be light, my lord, that you may bear it

Under a cloak that is of any length.

DUKE.

A cloak as long as thine will serve the turn?

VALENTINE.

Ay, my good lord.

DUKE.

Then let me see thy cloak.

I'll get me one of such another length.

VALENTINE.

Why, any cloak will serve the turn, my lord.

DUKE.

How shall I fashion me to wear a cloak?

I pray thee, let me feel thy cloak upon me.

[Pulls open VALENTINE'S cloak.]

What letter is this same? What's here?—'To Silvia'!

And here an engine fit for my proceeding!

I'll be so bold to break the seal for once.

'My thoughts do harbour with my Silvia nightly,

  And slaves they are to me, that send them flying.

O! could their master come and go as lightly,

   Himself would lodge where, senseless, they are lying!

My herald thoughts in thy pure bosom rest them,

   While I, their king, that thither them importune,

Do curse the grace that with such grace hath blest them,

   Because myself do want my servants' fortune.

I curse myself, for they are sent by me,

That they should harbour where their lord should be.'

What's here?

  'Silvia, this night I will enfranchise thee.'

'Tis so; and here's the ladder for the purpose.

Why, Phaethon—for thou art Merops' son—

Wilt thou aspire to guide the heavenly car,

And with thy daring folly burn the world?

Wilt thou reach stars because they shine on thee?

Go, base intruder! over-weening slave!

Bestow thy fawning smiles on equal mates,

And think my patience, more than thy desert,

Is privilege for thy departure hence.

Thank me for this more than for all the favours

Which, all too much, I have bestow'd on thee.

But if thou linger in my territories

Longer than swiftest expedition

Will give thee time to leave our royal court,

By heaven! my wrath shall far exceed the love

I ever bore my daughter or thyself.

Be gone! I will not hear thy vain excuse;

But, as thou lov'st thy life, make speed from hence.

[Exit.]

VALENTINE.

And why not death rather than living torment?

To die is to be banish'd from myself,

And Silvia is myself; banish'd from her

Is self from self,—a deadly banishment!

What light is light, if Silvia be not seen?

What joy is joy, if Silvia be not by?

Unless it be to think that she is by,

And feed upon the shadow of perfection.

Except I be by Silvia in the night,

There is no music in the nightingale;

Unless I look on Silvia in the day,

There is no day for me to look upon.

She is my essence, and I leave to be

If I be not by her fair influence

Foster'd, illumin'd, cherish'd, kept alive.

I fly not death, to fly his deadly doom:

Tarry I here, I but attend on death;

But fly I hence, I fly away from life.

[Enter PROTEUS and LAUNCE.]

PROTEUS.

Run, boy; run, run, seek him out.

LAUNCE.

Soho! soho!

PROTEUS.

What seest thou?

LAUNCE.

Him we go to find: there's not a hair on 's head but 'tis a

Valentine.

PROTEUS.

Valentine?

VALENTINE.

No.

PROTEUS.

Who then? his spirit?

VALENTINE.

Neither.

PROTEUS.

What then?

VALENTINE.

Nothing.

LAUNCE.

Can nothing speak? Master, shall I strike?

PROTEUS.

Who wouldst thou strike?

LAUNCE.

Nothing.

PROTEUS.

Villain, forbear.

LAUNCE.

Why, sir, I'll strike nothing. I pray you,—

PROTEUS.

Sirrah, I say, forbear.—Friend Valentine, a word.

VALENTINE.

My ears are stopp'd and cannot hear good news,

So much of bad already hath possess'd them.

PROTEUS.

Then in dumb silence will I bury mine,

For they are harsh, untuneable, and bad.

VALENTINE.

Is Silvia dead?

PROTEUS.

No, Valentine.

VALENTINE.

No Valentine, indeed, for sacred Silvia.

Hath she forsworn me?

PROTEUS.

No, Valentine.

VALENTINE.

No Valentine, if Silvia have forsworn me.

What is your news?

LAUNCE.

Sir, there is a proclamation that you are vanished.

PROTEUS.

That thou art banished, O, that's the news,

From hence, from Silvia, and from me thy friend.

VALENTINE.

O, I have fed upon this woe already,

And now excess of it will make me surfeit.

Doth Silvia know that I am banished?

PROTEUS.

Ay, ay; and she hath offer'd to the doom—

Which, unrevers'd, stands in effectual force—

A sea of melting pearl, which some call tears;

Those at her father's churlish feet she tender'd;

With them, upon her knees, her humble self,

Wringing her hands, whose whiteness so became them

As if but now they waxed pale for woe:

But neither bended knees, pure hands held up,

Sad sighs, deep groans, nor silver-shedding tears,

Could penetrate her uncompassionate sire;

But Valentine, if he be ta'en, must die.

Besides, her intercession chaf'd him so,

When she for thy repeal was suppliant,

That to close prison he commanded her,

With many bitter threats of biding there.

VALENTINE.

No more; unless the next word that thou speak'st

Have some malignant power upon my life:

If so, I pray thee breathe it in mine ear,

As ending anthem of my endless dolour.

PROTEUS.

Cease to lament for that thou canst not help,

And study help for that which thou lament'st.

Time is the nurse and breeder of all good.

Here if thou stay thou canst not see thy love;

Besides, thy staying will abridge thy life.

Hope is a lover's staff; walk hence with that

And manage it against despairing thoughts.

Thy letters may be here, though thou art hence,

Which, being writ to me, shall be deliver'd

Even in the milk-white bosom of thy love.

The time now serves not to expostulate:

Come, I'll convey thee through the city-gate;

And, ere I part with thee, confer at large

Of all that may concern thy love-affairs.

As thou lov'st Silvia, though not for thyself,

Regard thy danger, and along with me!

VALENTINE.

I pray thee, Launce, an if thou seest my boy,

Bid him make haste and meet me at the North-gate.

PROTEUS.

Go, sirrah, find him out. Come, Valentine.

VALENTINE.

O my dear Silvia! Hapless Valentine!

[Exeunt VALENTINE and PROTEUS.]

LAUNCE.

I am but a fool, look you, and yet I have the wit to think my master is a kind of a knave; but that's all one if he be but one knave. He lives not now that knows me to be in love; yet I am in love; but a team of horse shall not pluck that from me; nor who 'tis I love; and yet 'tis a woman; but what woman I will not tell myself; and yet 'tis a milkmaid; yet 'tis not a maid, for she hath had gossips; yet 'tis a maid, for she is her master's maid and serves for wages. She hath more qualities than a water-spaniel—which is much in a bare Christian.

[Pulling out a paper.]

Here is the catelog of her condition. 'Inprimis: She can fetch and carry.'
Why, a horse can do no more: nay, a horse cannot fetch, but only carry;
therefore is she better than a jade. 'Item: She can milk.' Look you, a sweet
virtue in a maid with clean hands.

[Enter SPEED.]

SPEED.

How now, Signior Launce! What news with your mastership?

LAUNCE.

With my master's ship? Why, it is at sea.

SPEED. Well, your old vice still: mistake the word. What news, then,
in your paper?

LAUNCE.

The blackest news that ever thou heardest.

SPEED.

Why, man? how black?

LAUNCE.

Why, as black as ink.

SPEED.

Let me read them.

LAUNCE.

Fie on thee, jolthead! thou canst not read.

SPEED.

Thou liest; I can.

LAUNCE.

I will try thee. Tell me this: who begot thee?

SPEED.

Marry, the son of my grandfather.

LAUNCE.

O, illiterate loiterer! It was the son of thy grandmother.

This proves that thou canst not read.

SPEED.

Come, fool, come; try me in thy paper.

LAUNCE.

There; and Saint Nicholas be thy speed!

SPEED.

'Inprimis, She can milk.'

LAUNCE.

Ay, that she can.

SPEED.

'Item, She brews good ale.'

LAUNCE. And thereof comes the proverb, 'Blessing of your heart, you brew good ale.'

SPEED.

'Item, She can sew.'

LAUNCE.

That's as much as to say 'Can she so?'

SPEED.

'Item, She can knit.'

LAUNCE. What need a man care for a stock with a wench, when she can knit him a stock?

SPEED.

'Item, She can wash and scour.'

LAUNCE.

A special virtue; for then she need not be washed and scoured.

SPEED.

'Item, She can spin.'

LAUNCE. Then may I set the world on wheels, when she can spin for her living.

SPEED.

'Item, She hath many nameless virtues.'

LAUNCE. That's as much as to say, bastard virtues; that indeed know not their fathers, and therefore have no names.

SPEED.

'Here follow her vices.'

LAUNCE.

Close at the heels of her virtues.

SPEED. 'Item, She is not to be kissed fasting, in respect of her breath.'

LAUNCE.

Well, that fault may be mended with a breakfast.

Read on.

SPEED.

'Item, She hath a sweet mouth.'

LAUNCE.

That makes amends for her sour breath.

SPEED.

'Item, She doth talk in her sleep.'

LAUNCE.

It's no matter for that, so she sleep not in her talk.

SPEED.

'Item, She is slow in words.'

LAUNCE. O villain, that set this down among her vices! To be slow in words is a woman's only virtue. I pray thee, out with't; and place it for her chief virtue.

SPEED.

'Item, She is proud.'

LAUNCE. Out with that too: it was Eve's legacy, and cannot be ta'en from her.

SPEED.

'Item, She hath no teeth.'

LAUNCE.

I care not for that neither, because I love crusts.

SPEED.

'Item, She is curst.'

LAUNCE.

Well; the best is, she hath no teeth to bite.

SPEED.

'Item, She will often praise her liquor.'

LAUNCE. If her liquor be good, she shall: if she will not, I will; for good things should be praised.

SPEED.

'Item, She is too liberal.'

LAUNCE. Of her tongue she cannot, for that's writ down she is slow of; of her purse she shall not, for that I'll keep shut. Now of another thing she may, and that cannot I help. Well, proceed.

SPEED. 'Item, She hath more hair than wit, and more faults than hairs, and more wealth than faults.'

LAUNCE. Stop there; I'll have her; she was mine, and not mine, twice or thrice in that last article. Rehearse that once more.

SPEED.

'Item, She hath more hair than wit'—

LAUNCE. More hair than wit it may be; I'll prove it: the cover of the salt hides the salt, and therefore it is more than the salt; the hair that covers the wit is more than the wit, for the greater hides the less. What's next?

SPEED.

'And more faults than hairs.'—

LAUNCE.

That's monstrous! O, that that were out!

SPEED.

'And more wealth than faults.'

LAUNCE. Why, that word makes the faults gracious. Well, I'll have her; an if it be a match, as nothing is impossible,—

SPEED.

What then?

LAUNCE. Why, then will I tell thee,—that thy master stays for thee at the North-gate.

SPEED.

For me?

LAUNCE. For thee! ay, who art thou? He hath stay'd for a better man than thee.

SPEED.

And must I go to him?

LAUNCE. Thou must run to him, for thou hast stayed so long that going will scarce serve the turn.

SPEED.

Why didst not tell me sooner? Pox of your love letters!

[Exit.]

LAUNCE. Now will he be swing'd for reading my letter. An unmannerly slave that will thrust himself into secrets! I'll after, to rejoice in the boy's correction.

[Exit.]

SCENE 2. The same. A room in the DUKE'S palace.

[Enter DUKE and THURIO.]

DUKE.

Sir Thurio, fear not but that she will love you

Now Valentine is banish'd from her sight.

THURIO.

Since his exile she hath despis'd me most,

Forsworn my company and rail'd at me,

That I am desperate of obtaining her.

DUKE.

This weak impress of love is as a figure

Trenched in ice, which with an hour's heat

Dissolves to water and doth lose his form.

A little time will melt her frozen thoughts,

And worthless Valentine shall be forgot.

[Enter PROTEUS.]

How now, Sir Proteus! Is your countryman,

According to our proclamation, gone?

PROTEUS.

Gone, my good lord.

DUKE.

My daughter takes his going grievously.

PROTEUS.

A little time, my lord, will kill that grief.

DUKE.

So I believe; but Thurio thinks not so.

Proteus, the good conceit I hold of thee,—

For thou hast shown some sign of good desert,—

Makes me the better to confer with thee.

PROTEUS.

Longer than I prove loyal to your Grace

Let me not live to look upon your Grace.

DUKE.

Thou know'st how willingly I would effect

The match between Sir Thurio and my daughter.

PROTEUS.

I do, my lord.

DUKE.

And also, I think, thou art not ignorant

How she opposes her against my will.

PROTEUS.

She did, my lord, when Valentine was here.

DUKE.

Ay, and perversely she persevers so.

What might we do to make the girl forget

The love of Valentine, and love Sir Thurio?

PROTEUS.

The best way is to slander Valentine

With falsehood, cowardice, and poor descent,

Three things that women highly hold in hate.

DUKE.

Ay, but she'll think that it is spoke in hate.

PROTEUS.

Ay, if his enemy deliver it;

Therefore it must with circumstance be spoken

By one whom she esteemeth as his friend.

DUKE.

Then you must undertake to slander him.

PROTEUS.

And that, my lord, I shall be loath to do:

'Tis an ill office for a gentleman,

Especially against his very friend.

DUKE.

Where your good word cannot advantage him,

Your slander never can endamage him;

Therefore the office is indifferent,

Being entreated to it by your friend.

PROTEUS.

You have prevail'd, my lord; if I can do it

By aught that I can speak in his dispraise,

She shall not long continue love to him.

But say this weed her love from Valentine,

It follows not that she will love Sir Thurio.

THURIO.

Therefore, as you unwind her love from him,

Lest it should ravel and be good to none,

You must provide to bottom it on me;

Which must be done by praising me as much

As you in worth dispraise Sir Valentine.

DUKE.

And, Proteus, we dare trust you in this kind,

Because we know, on Valentine's report,

You are already Love's firm votary

And cannot soon revolt and change your mind.

Upon this warrant shall you have access

Where you with Silvia may confer at large;

For she is lumpish, heavy, melancholy,

And, for your friend's sake, will be glad of you;

Where you may temper her by your persuasion

To hate young Valentine and love my friend.

PROTEUS.

As much as I can do I will effect.

But you, Sir Thurio, are not sharp enough;

You must lay lime to tangle her desires

By wailful sonnets, whose composed rhymes

Should be full-fraught with serviceable vows.

DUKE.

Ay,

Much is the force of heaven-bred poesy.

PROTEUS.

Say that upon the altar of her beauty

You sacrifice your tears, your sighs, your heart.

Write till your ink be dry, and with your tears

Moist it again, and frame some feeling line

That may discover such integrity:

For Orpheus' lute was strung with poets' sinews,

Whose golden touch could soften steel and stones,

Make tigers tame, and huge leviathans

Forsake unsounded deeps to dance on sands.

After your dire-lamenting elegies,

Visit by night your lady's chamber-window

With some sweet consort: to their instruments

Tune a deploring dump; the night's dead silence

Will well become such sweet-complaining grievance.

This, or else nothing, will inherit her.

DUKE.

This discipline shows thou hast been in love.

THURIO.

And thy advice this night I'll put in practice.

Therefore, sweet Proteus, my direction-giver,

Let us into the city presently

To sort some gentlemen well skill'd in music.

I have a sonnet that will serve the turn

To give the onset to thy good advice.

DUKE.

About it, gentlemen!

PROTEUS.

We'll wait upon your Grace till after-supper,

And afterward determine our proceedings.

DUKE.

Even now about it! I will pardon you.

[Exeunt.]

ACT 4.

SCENE 1. A forest between Milan and Verona.

[Enter certain OUTLAWS.]

FIRST OUTLAW.

Fellows, stand fast; I see a passenger.

SECOND OUTLAW.

If there be ten, shrink not, but down with 'em.

[Enter VALENTINE and SPEED.]

THIRD OUTLAW.

Stand, sir, and throw us that you have about ye;

If not, we'll make you sit, and rifle you.

SPEED.

Sir, we are undone: these are the villains

That all the travellers do fear so much.

VALENTINE.

My friends,—

FIRST OUTLAW.

That's not so, sir; we are your enemies.

SECOND OUTLAW.

Peace! we'll hear him.

THIRD OUTLAW.

Ay, by my beard, will we, for he is a proper man.

VALENTINE.

Then know that I have little wealth to lose;

A man I am cross'd with adversity;

My riches are these poor habiliments,

Of which if you should here disfurnish me,

You take the sum and substance that I have.

SECOND OUTLAW.

Whither travel you?

VALENTINE.

To Verona.

FIRST OUTLAW.

Whence came you?

VALENTINE.

From Milan.

THIRD OUTLAW.

Have you long sojourn'd there?

VALENTINE.

Some sixteen months, and longer might have stay'd,

If crooked fortune had not thwarted me.

FIRST OUTLAW.

What! were you banish'd thence?

VALENTINE.

I was.

SECOND OUTLAW.

For what offence?

VALENTINE.

For that which now torments me to rehearse:

I kill'd a man, whose death I much repent;

But yet I slew him manfully in fight,

Without false vantage or base treachery.

FIRST OUTLAW.

Why, ne'er repent it, if it were done so.

But were you banish'd for so small a fault?

VALENTINE.

I was, and held me glad of such a doom.

SECOND OUTLAW.

Have you the tongues?

VALENTINE.

My youthful travel therein made me happy,

Or else I often had been miserable.

THIRD OUTLAW.

By the bare scalp of Robin Hood's fat friar,

This fellow were a king for our wild faction!

FIRST OUTLAW.

We'll have him: Sirs, a word.

SPEED.

Master, be one of them; it's an honourable kind of thievery.

VALENTINE.

Peace, villain!

SECOND OUTLAW.

Tell us this: have you anything to take to?

VALENTINE.

Nothing but my fortune.

THIRD OUTLAW.

Know, then, that some of us are gentlemen,

Such as the fury of ungovern'd youth

Thrust from the company of awful men:

Myself was from Verona banished

For practising to steal away a lady,

An heir, and near allied unto the duke.

SECOND OUTLAW.

And I from Mantua, for a gentleman

Who, in my mood, I stabb'd unto the heart.

FIRST OUTLAW.

And I for such-like petty crimes as these.

But to the purpose; for we cite our faults,

That they may hold excus'd our lawless lives;

And, partly, seeing you are beautified

With goodly shape, and by your own report

A linguist, and a man of such perfection

As we do in our quality much want—

SECOND OUTLAW.

Indeed, because you are a banish'd man,

Therefore, above the rest, we parley to you.

Are you content to be our general?

To make a virtue of necessity

And live as we do in this wilderness?

THIRD OUTLAW.

What say'st thou? Wilt thou be of our consort?

Say 'ay' and be the captain of us all:

We'll do thee homage, and be rul'd by thee,

Love thee as our commander and our king.

FIRST OUTLAW.

But if thou scorn our courtesy thou diest.

SECOND OUTLAW.

Thou shalt not live to brag what we have offer'd.

VALENTINE.

I take your offer, and will live with you,

Provided that you do no outrages

On silly women or poor passengers.

THIRD OUTLAW.

No, we detest such vile base practices.

Come, go with us; we'll bring thee to our crews,

And show thee all the treasure we have got;

Which, with ourselves, all rest at thy dispose.

[Exeunt.]

SCENE 2. Milan. The sourt of the DUKE'S palace.

[Enter PROTEUS.]

PROTEUS.

Already have I been false to Valentine,

And now I must be as unjust to Thurio.

Under the colour of commending him,

I have access my own love to prefer:

But Silvia is too fair, too true, too holy,

To be corrupted with my worthless gifts.

When I protest true loyalty to her,

She twits me with my falsehood to my friend;

When to her beauty I commend my vows,

She bids me think how I have been forsworn

In breaking faith with Julia whom I lov'd;

And notwithstanding all her sudden quips,

The least whereof would quell a lover's hope,

Yet, spaniel-like, the more she spurns my love

The more it grows and fawneth on her still.

But here comes Thurio. Now must we to her window,

And give some evening music to her ear.

[Enter THURIO and Musicians.]

THURIO.

How now, Sir Proteus! are you crept before us?

PROTEUS.

Ay, gentle Thurio; for you know that love

Will creep in service where it cannot go.

THURIO.

Ay, but I hope, sir, that you love not here.

PROTEUS.

Sir, but I do; or else I would be hence.

THURIO.

Who? Silvia?

PROTEUS.

Ay, Silvia, for your sake.

THURIO.

I thank you for your own. Now, gentlemen,

Let's tune, and to it lustily awhile.

[Enter Host, and JULIA in boy's clothes.]

HOST. Now, my young guest, methinks you're allycholly; I pray you, why is it?

JULIA.

Marry, mine host, because I cannot be merry.

HOST. Come, we'll have you merry; I'll bring you where you shall hear music, and see the gentleman that you asked for.

JULIA.

But shall I hear him speak?

HOST.

Ay, that you shall.

JULIA.

That will be music.

[Music plays.]

HOST.

Hark! hark!

JULIA.

Is he among these?

HOST.

Ay; but peace! let's hear 'em.

[SONG]

Who is Silvia? What is she,

That all our swains commend her?

Holy, fair, and wise is she;

The heaven such grace did lend her,

That she might admired be.

Is she kind as she is fair?

For beauty lives with kindness.

Love doth to her eyes repair,

To help him of his blindness;

And, being help'd, inhabits there.

Then to Silvia let us sing

That Silvia is excelling;

She excels each mortal thing

Upon the dull earth dwelling.

' To her let us garlands bring.

HOST.

How now, are you sadder than you were before?

How do you, man? The music likes you not.

JULIA.

You mistake; the musician likes me not.

HOST.

Why, my pretty youth?

JULIA.

He plays false, father.

HOST.

How? out of tune on the strings?

JULIA. Not so; but yet so false that he grieves my very heart-strings.

HOST.

You have a quick ear.

JULIA.

Ay, I would I were deaf; it makes me have a slow heart.

HOST.

I perceive you delight not in music.

JULIA.

Not a whit,—when it jars so.

HOST.

Hark! what fine change is in the music!

JULIA.

Ay, that change is the spite.

HOST.

You would have them always play but one thing?

JULIA.

I would always have one play but one thing.

But, Host, doth this Sir Proteus, that we talk on,

Often resort unto this gentlewoman?

HOST. I tell you what Launce, his man, told me: he lov'd her out of all nick.

JULIA.

Where is Launce?

HOST. Gone to seek his dog, which to-morrow, by his master's command, he must carry for a present to his lady.

JULIA.

Peace! stand aside: the company parts.

PROTEUS.

Sir Thurio, fear not you; I will so plead

That you shall say my cunning drift excels.

THURIO.

Where meet we?

PROTEUS.

At Saint Gregory's well.

THURIO.

Farewell.

[Exeunt THURIO and Musicians.]

[Enter SILVIA above, at her window.]

PROTEUS.

Madam, good even to your ladyship.

SILVIA.

I thank you for your music, gentlemen.

Who is that that spake?

PROTEUS.

One, lady, if you knew his pure heart's truth,

You would quickly learn to know him by his voice.

SILVIA.

Sir Proteus, as I take it.

PROTEUS.

Sir Proteus, gentle lady, and your servant.

SILVIA.

What's your will?

PROTEUS.

That I may compass yours.

SILVIA.

You have your wish; my will is even this,

That presently you hie you home to bed.

Thou subtle, perjur'd, false, disloyal man!

Think'st thou I am so shallow, so conceitless,

To be seduced by thy flattery,

That hast deceiv'd so many with thy vows?

Return, return, and make thy love amends.

For me, by this pale queen of night I swear,

I am so far from granting thy request

That I despise thee for thy wrongful suit,

And by and by intend to chide myself

Even for this time I spend in talking to thee.

PROTEUS.

I grant, sweet love, that I did love a lady;

But she is dead.

JULIA.

[Aside] 'Twere false, if I should speak it;

For I am sure she is not buried.

SILVIA.

Say that she be; yet Valentine, thy friend,

Survives, to whom, thyself art witness,

I am betroth'd; and art thou not asham'd

To wrong him with thy importunacy?

PROTEUS.

I likewise hear that Valentine is dead.

SILVIA.

And so suppose am I; for in his grave,

Assure thyself my love is buried.

PROTEUS.

Sweet lady, let me rake it from the earth.

SILVIA.

Go to thy lady's grave, and call hers thence;

Or, at the least, in hers sepulchre thine.

JULIA.

[Aside] He heard not that.

PROTEUS.

Madam, if your heart be so obdurate,

Vouchsafe me yet your picture for my love,

The picture that is hanging in your chamber;

To that I'll speak, to that I'll sigh and weep;

For, since the substance of your perfect self

Is else devoted, I am but a shadow;

And to your shadow will I make true love.

JULIA.

[Aside] If 'twere a substance, you would, sure, deceive it

And make it but a shadow, as I am.

SILVIA.

I am very loath to be your idol, sir;

But since your falsehood shall become you well

To worship shadows and adore false shapes,

Send to me in the morning, and I'll send it;

And so, good rest.

PROTEUS.

As wretches have o'ernight

That wait for execution in the morn.

[Exeunt PROTEUS and SILVIA, above.]

JULIA.

Host, will you go?

HOST.

By my halidom, I was fast asleep.

JULIA.

Pray you, where lies Sir Proteus?

HOST.

Marry, at my house. Trust me, I think 'tis almost day.

JULIA.

Not so; but it hath been the longest night

That e'er I watch'd, and the most heaviest.

[Exeunt.]

SCENE 3. The same.

[Enter EGLAMOUR.]

EGLAMOUR.

This is the hour that Madam Silvia

Entreated me to call and know her mind:

There's some great matter she'd employ me in.

Madam, madam!

[Enter SILVIA above, at her window.]

SILVIA.

Who calls?

EGLAMOUR.

Your servant and your friend;

One that attends your ladyship's command.

SILVIA.

Sir Eglamour, a thousand times good morrow.

EGLAMOUR.

As many, worthy lady, to yourself.

According to your ladyship's impose,

I am thus early come to know what service

It is your pleasure to command me in.

SILVIA.

O Eglamour, thou art a gentleman—

Think not I flatter, for I swear I do not—

Valiant, wise, remorseful, well accomplish'd.

Thou art not ignorant what dear good will

I bear unto the banish'd Valentine;

Nor how my father would enforce me marry

Vain Thurio, whom my very soul abhors.

Thyself hast lov'd; and I have heard thee say

No grief did ever come so near thy heart

As when thy lady and thy true love died,

Upon whose grave thou vow'dst pure chastity.

Sir Eglamour, I would to Valentine,

To Mantua, where I hear he makes abode;

And, for the ways are dangerous to pass,

I do desire thy worthy company,

Upon whose faith and honour I repose.

Urge not my father's anger, Eglamour,

But think upon my grief, a lady's grief,

And on the justice of my flying hence,

To keep me from a most unholy match,

Which heaven and fortune still rewards with plagues.

I do desire thee, even from a heart

As full of sorrows as the sea of sands,

To bear me company and go with me;

If not, to hide what I have said to thee,

That I may venture to depart alone.

EGLAMOUR.

Madam, I pity much your grievances;

Which since I know they virtuously are plac'd,

I give consent to go along with you,

Recking as little what betideth me

As much I wish all good befortune you.

When will you go?

SILVIA.

This evening coming.

EGLAMOUR.

Where shall I meet you?

SILVIA.

At Friar Patrick's cell,

Where I intend holy confession.

EGLAMOUR.

I will not fail your ladyship. Good morrow, gentle lady.

SILVIA.

Good morrow, kind Sir Eglamour.

[Exeunt severally.]

SCENE 4. The same.

[Enter LAUNCE with his dog.]

LAUNCE. When a man's servant shall play the cur with him, look you, it goes hard; one that I brought up of a puppy; one that I saved from drowning, when three or four of his blind brothers and sisters went to it. I have taught him, even as one would say precisely 'Thus I would teach a dog.' I was sent to deliver him as a present to Mistress Silvia from my master; and I came no sooner into the dining-chamber, but he steps me to her trencher and steals her capon's leg. O! 'tis a foul thing when a cur cannot keep himself in all companies! I would have, as one should say, one that takes upon him to be a dog indeed, to be, as it were, a dog at all things. If I had not had more wit than he, to take a fault upon me that he did, I think verily he had been hang'd for't; sure as I live, he had suffer'd for't; you shall judge. He thrusts me himself into the company of three or four gentleman-like dogs under the duke's table; he had not been there—bless the mark, a pissing-while, but all the chamber smelt him. 'Out with the dog!' says one; 'What cur is that?' says another; 'Whip him out' says the third; 'Hang him up' says the duke. I, having been acquainted with the smell before, knew it was Crab, and goes me to the fellow that whips the dogs: 'Friend,' quoth I 'you mean to whip the dog?' 'Ay, marry do I,' quoth he. 'You do him the more wrong,' quoth I; ''twas I did the thing you wot of.' He makes me no more ado, but whips me out of the chamber. How many masters would do this for his servant? Nay, I'll be sworn, I have sat in the stock for puddings he hath stolen, otherwise he had been executed; I have stood on the pillory for geese he hath killed, otherwise he had suffered for't. Thou think'st not of this now. Nay, I remember the trick you serv'd me when I took my leave of Madam Silvia: did not I bid thee still mark me and do as I do? When didst thou see me heave up my leg and make water against a gentlewoman's farthingale? Didst thou ever see me do such a trick?

[Enter PROTEUS, and JULIA in boy's clothes.]

PROTEUS.

Sebastian is thy name? I like thee well,

And will employ thee in some service presently.

JULIA.

In what you please; I'll do what I can.

PROTEUS.

I hope thou wilt.

[To LAUNCE] How now, you whoreson peasant!

Where have you been these two days loitering?

LAUNCE.

Marry, sir, I carried Mistress Silvia the dog you bade me.

PROTEUS.

And what says she to my little jewel?

LAUNCE. Marry, she says your dog was a cur, and tells you currish thanks is good enough for such a present.

PROTEUS.

But she received my dog?

LAUNCE. No, indeed, did she not: here have I brought him back again.

PROTEUS.

What! didst thou offer her this from me?

LAUNCE. Ay, sir; the other squirrel was stolen from me by the hangman boys in the market-place; and then I offered her mine own, who is a dog as big as ten of yours, and therefore the gift the greater.

PROTEUS.

Go, get thee hence and find my dog again,

Or ne'er return again into my sight.

Away, I say. Stayest thou to vex me here?

A slave that still an end turns me to shame!

[Exit LAUNCE.]

Sebastian, I have entertained thee

Partly that I have need of such a youth

That can with some discretion do my business,

For 'tis no trusting to yond foolish lout;

But chiefly for thy face and thy behaviour,

Which, if my augury deceive me not,

Witness good bringing up, fortune, and truth:

Therefore, know thou, for this I entertain thee.

Go presently, and take this ring with thee,

Deliver it to Madam Silvia:

She lov'd me well deliver'd it to me.

JULIA.

It seems you lov'd not her, to leave her token.

She's dead, belike?

PROTEUS.

Not so: I think she lives.

JULIA.

Alas!

PROTEUS.

Why dost thou cry 'Alas'?

JULIA.

I cannot choose

But pity her.

PROTEUS.

Wherefore shouldst thou pity her?

JULIA.

Because methinks that she lov'd you as well

As you do love your lady Silvia.

She dreams on him that has forgot her love:

You dote on her that cares not for your love.

'Tis pity love should be so contrary;

And thinking on it makes me cry 'alas!'

PROTEUS.

Well, give her that ring, and therewithal

This letter: that's her chamber. Tell my lady

I claim the promise for her heavenly picture.

Your message done, hie home unto my chamber,

Where thou shalt find me sad and solitary.

[Exit.]

JULIA.

How many women would do such a message?

Alas, poor Proteus! thou hast entertain'd

A fox to be the shepherd of thy lambs.

Alas, poor fool! why do I pity him

That with his very heart despiseth me?

Because he loves her, he despiseth me;

Because I love him, I must pity him.

This ring I gave him, when he parted from me,

To bind him to remember my good will;

And now am I—unhappy messenger—

To plead for that which I would not obtain,

To carry that which I would have refus'd,

To praise his faith, which I would have disprais'd.

I am my master's true-confirmed love,

But cannot be true servant to my master

Unless I prove false traitor to myself.

Yet will I woo for him, but yet so coldly

As, heaven it knows, I would not have him speed.

[Enter SILVIA, attended.]

Gentlewoman, good day! I pray you be my mean

To bring me where to speak with Madam Silvia.

SILVIA.

What would you with her, if that I be she?

JULIA.

If you be she, I do entreat your patience

To hear me speak the message I am sent on.

SILVIA.

From whom?

JULIA.

From my master, Sir Proteus, madam.

SILVIA.

O! he sends you for a picture?

JULIA.

Ay, madam.

SILVIA.

Ursula, bring my picture there.

[A picture brought.]

Go, give your master this. Tell him from me,

One Julia, that his changing thoughts forget,

Would better fit his chamber than this shadow.

JULIA.

Madam, please you peruse this letter.—

Pardon me, madam; I have unadvis'd

Deliver'd you a paper that I should not:

This is the letter to your ladyship.

SILVIA.

I pray thee, let me look on that again.

JULIA.

It may not be: good madam, pardon me.

SILVIA.

There, hold.

I will not look upon your master's lines:

I know they are stuff'd with protestations

And full of new-found oaths, which he will break

As easily as I do tear his paper.

JULIA.

Madam, he sends your ladyship this ring.

SILVIA.

The more shame for him that he sends it me;

For I have heard him say a thousand times

His Julia gave it him at his departure.

Though his false finger have profan'd the ring,

Mine shall not do his Julia so much wrong.

JULIA.

She thanks you.

SILVIA.

What say'st thou?

JULIA.

I thank you, madam, that you tender her.

Poor gentlewoman, my master wrongs her much.

SILVIA.

Dost thou know her?

JULIA.

Almost as well as I do know myself:

To think upon her woes, I do protest

That I have wept a hundred several times.

SILVIA.

Belike she thinks, that Proteus hath forsook her.

JULIA.

I think she doth, and that's her cause of sorrow.

SILVIA.

Is she not passing fair?

JULIA.

She hath been fairer, madam, than she is.

When she did think my master lov'd her well,

She, in my judgment, was as fair as you;

But since she did neglect her looking-glass

And threw her sun-expelling mask away,

The air hath starv'd the roses in her cheeks

And pinch'd the lily-tincture of her face,

That now she is become as black as I.

SILVIA.

How tall was she?

JULIA.

About my stature; for at Pentecost,

When all our pageants of delight were play'd,

Our youth got me to play the woman's part,

And I was trimm'd in Madam Julia's gown,

Which served me as fit, by all men's judgments,

As if the garment had been made for me:

Therefore I know she is about my height.

And at that time I made her weep agood;

For I did play a lamentable part.

Madam, 'twas Ariadne passioning

For Theseus' perjury and unjust flight;

Which I so lively acted with my tears

That my poor mistress, mov'd therewithal,

Wept bitterly; and would I might be dead

If I in thought felt not her very sorrow!

SILVIA.

She is beholding to thee, gentle youth.—

Alas, poor lady, desolate and left!

I weep myself, to think upon thy words.

Here, youth, there is my purse; I give thee this

For thy sweet mistress' sake, because thou lov'st her.

Farewell.

JULIA.

And she shall thank you for't, if e'er you know her.—

[Exit SILVIA with ATTENDANTS]

A virtuous gentlewoman, mild and beautiful!

I hope my master's suit will be but cold,

Since she respects my mistress' love so much.

Alas, how love can trifle with itself!

Here is her picture; let me see. I think,

If I had such a tire, this face of mine

Were full as lovely as is this of hers;

And yet the painter flatter'd her a little,

Unless I flatter with myself too much.

Her hair is auburn, mine is perfect yellow:

If that be all the difference in his love,

I'll get me such a colour'd periwig.

Her eyes are grey as glass, and so are mine;

Ay, but her forehead's low, and mine's as high.

What should it be that he respects in her

But I can make respective in myself,

If this fond Love were not a blinded god?

Come, shadow, come, and take this shadow up,

For 'tis thy rival. O thou senseless form!

Thou shalt be worshipp'd, kiss'd, lov'd, and ador'd,

And, were there sense in his idolatry,

My substance should be statue in thy stead.

I'll use thee kindly for thy mistress' sake,

That us'd me so; or else, by Jove I vow,

I should have scratch'd out your unseeing eyes,

To make my master out of love with thee.

[Exit.]

ACT 5.

SCENE I. Milan. An abbey

[Enter EGLAMOUR.]

EGLAMOUR.

The sun begins to gild the western sky,

And now it is about the very hour

That Silvia at Friar Patrick's cell should meet me.

She will not fail; for lovers break not hours

Unless it be to come before their time,

So much they spur their expedition.

See, where she comes.

[Enter SILVIA.]

Lady, a happy evening!

SILVIA.

Amen, amen! Go on, good Eglamour,

Out at the postern by the abbey wall.

I fear I am attended by some spies.

EGLAMOUR.

Fear not: the forest is not three leagues off;

If we recover that, we are sure enough.

[Exeunt.]

SCENE 2. The same. A room in the DUKE'S palace.

[Enter THURIO, PROTEUS, and JULIA.]

THURIO.

Sir Proteus, what says Silvia to my suit?

PROTEUS.

O, sir, I find her milder than she was;

And yet she takes exceptions at your person.

THURIO.

What! that my leg is too long?

PROTEUS.

No; that it is too little.

THURIO.

I'll wear a boot to make it somewhat rounder.

JULIA.

[Aside] But love will not be spurr'd to what it loathes.

THURIO.

What says she to my face?

PROTEUS.

She says it is a fair one.

THURIO.

Nay, then, the wanton lies; my face is black.

PROTEUS.

But pearls are fair; and the old saying is:

'Black men are pearls in beauteous ladies' eyes.'

JULIA.

[Aside] 'Tis true, such pearls as put out ladies' eyes;

For I had rather wink than look on them.

THURIO.

How likes she my discourse?

PROTEUS.

Ill, when you talk of war.

THURIO.

But well when I discourse of love and peace?

JULIA.

[Aside] But better, indeed, when you hold your peace.

THURIO.

What says she to my valour?

PROTEUS.

O, sir, she makes no doubt of that.

JULIA.

[Aside] She needs not, when she knows it cowardice.

THURIO.

What says she to my birth?

PROTEUS.

That you are well deriv'd.

JULIA.

[Aside] True; from a gentleman to a fool.

THURIO.

Considers she my possessions?

PROTEUS.

O, ay; and pities them.

THURIO.

Wherefore?

JULIA.

[Aside] That such an ass should owe them.

PROTEUS.

That they are out by lease.

JULIA.

Here comes the duke.

[Enter DUKE.]

DUKE.

How now, Sir Proteus! how now, Thurio!

Which of you saw Sir Eglamour of late?

THURIO.

Not I.

PROTEUS.

Nor I.

DUKE.

Saw you my daughter?

PROTEUS.

Neither.

DUKE.

Why then,

She's fled unto that peasant Valentine;

And Eglamour is in her company.

'Tis true; for Friar Lawrence met them both

As he in penance wander'd through the forest;

Him he knew well, and guess'd that it was she,

But, being mask'd, he was not sure of it;

Besides, she did intend confession

At Patrick's cell this even; and there she was not.

These likelihoods confirm her flight from hence.

Therefore, I pray you, stand not to discourse,

But mount you presently, and meet with me

Upon the rising of the mountain-foot

That leads toward Mantua, whither they are fled.

Dispatch, sweet gentlemen, and follow me.

[Exit.]

THURIO.

Why, this it is to be a peevish girl

That flies her fortune when it follows her.

135

I'll after, more to be reveng'd on Eglamour

Than for the love of reckless Silvia.

[Exit.]

PROTEUS.

And I will follow, more for Silvia's love

Than hate of Eglamour, that goes with her.

[Exit.]

JULIA.

And I will follow, more to cross that love

Than hate for Silvia, that is gone for love.

[Exit.]

SCENE 3. Frontiers of Mantua. The forest.

[Enter OUTLAWS with SILVA.]

FIRST OUTLAW.

Come, come.

Be patient; we must bring you to our captain.

SILVIA.

A thousand more mischances than this one

Have learn'd me how to brook this patiently.

SECOND OUTLAW.

Come, bring her away.

FIRST OUTLAW.

Where is the gentleman that was with her?

SECOND OUTLAW.

Being nimble-footed, he hath outrun us;

But Moyses and Valerius follow him.

Go thou with her to the west end of the wood;

There is our captain; we'll follow him that's fled.

The thicket is beset; he cannot 'scape.

[Exeunt all except the First Outlaw and SYLVIA.]

FIRST OUTLAW.

Come, I must bring you to our captain's cave.

Fear not; he bears an honourable mind,

And will not use a woman lawlessly.

SILVIA.

O Valentine, this I endure for thee!

[Exeunt.]

SCENE 4. Another part of the forest.

[Enter VALENTINE.]

VALENTINE.

How use doth breed a habit in a man!

This shadowy desert, unfrequented woods,

I better brook than flourishing peopled towns.

Here can I sit alone, unseen of any,

And to the nightingale's complaining notes

Tune my distresses and record my woes.

O thou that dost inhabit in my breast,

Leave not the mansion so long tenantless,

Lest, growing ruinous, the building fall

And leave no memory of what it was!

Repair me with thy presence, Silvia!

Thou gentle nymph, cherish thy forlorn swain. [Noise within.]

What halloing and what stir is this to-day?

These are my mates, that make their wills their law,

Have some unhappy passenger in chase.

They love me well; yet I have much to do

To keep them from uncivil outrages.

Withdraw thee, Valentine: who's this comes here?

[Steps aside.]

[Enter PROTEUS, SILVIA, and JULIA.]

PROTEUS.

Madam, this service I have done for you—

Though you respect not aught your servant doth—

To hazard life, and rescue you from him

That would have forc'd your honour and your love.

Vouchsafe me, for my meed, but one fair look;

A smaller boon than this I cannot beg,

And less than this, I am sure, you cannot give.

VALENTINE. [Aside] How like a dream is this I see and hear!

Love, lend me patience to forbear awhile.

SILVIA.

O miserable, unhappy that I am!

PROTEUS.

Unhappy were you, madam, ere I came;

But by my coming I have made you happy.

SILVIA.

By thy approach thou mak'st me most unhappy.

JULIA. [Aside] And me, when he approacheth to your presence.

SILVIA.

Had I been seized by a hungry lion,

I would have been a breakfast to the beast,

Rather than have false Proteus rescue me.

O! heaven be judge how I love Valentine,

Whose life's as tender to me as my soul,

And full as much—for more there cannot be—

I do detest false, perjur'd Proteus.

Therefore be gone; solicit me no more.

PROTEUS.

What dangerous action, stood it next to death,

Would I not undergo for one calm look!

O, 'tis the curse in love, and still approv'd,

When women cannot love where they're belov'd!

SILVIA.

When Proteus cannot love where he's belov'd!

Read over Julia's heart, thy first best love,

For whose dear sake thou didst then rend thy faith

Into a thousand oaths; and all those oaths

Descended into perjury, to love me.

Thou hast no faith left now, unless thou'dst two,

And that's far worse than none: better have none

Than plural faith, which is too much by one.

Thou counterfeit to thy true friend!

PROTEUS.

In love,

Who respects friend?

SILVIA.

All men but Proteus.

PROTEUS.

Nay, if the gentle spirit of moving words

Can no way change you to a milder form,

I'll woo you like a soldier, at arms' end,

And love you 'gainst the nature of love,—force ye.

SILVIA.

O heaven!

PROTEUS.

I'll force thee yield to my desire.

VALENTINE. [Coming forward.]

Ruffian! let go that rude uncivil touch;

Thou friend of an ill fashion!

PROTEUS.

Valentine!

VALENTINE.

Thou common friend, that's without faith or love—

For such is a friend now—treacherous man,

Thou hast beguil'd my hopes; nought but mine eye

Could have persuaded me. Now I dare not say

I have one friend alive: thou wouldst disprove me.

Who should be trusted, when one's own right hand

Is perjur'd to the bosom? Proteus,

I am sorry I must never trust thee more,

But count the world a stranger for thy sake.

The private wound is deep'st. O time most curst!

'Mongst all foes that a friend should be the worst!

PROTEUS.

My shame and guilt confounds me.

Forgive me, Valentine; if hearty sorrow

Be a sufficient ransom for offence,

I tender 't here; I do as truly suffer

As e'er I did commit.

VALENTINE.

Then I am paid;

And once again I do receive thee honest.

Who by repentance is not satisfied

Is nor of heaven nor earth, for these are pleas'd.

By penitence the Eternal's wrath's appeas'd:

And, that my love may appear plain and free,

All that was mine in Silvia I give thee.

JULIA.

O me unhappy! [Swoons]

PROTEUS.

Look to the boy.

VALENTINE.

Why, boy! why, wag! how now!

What's the matter? Look up; speak.

JULIA.

O good sir, my master charg'd me to deliver a ring to Madam

Silvia, which, out of my neglect, was never done.

PROTEUS.

Where is that ring, boy?

JULIA.

Here 'tis; this is it. [Gives a ring.]

PROTEUS.

How! let me see. Why, this is the ring I gave to Julia.

JULIA.

O, cry you mercy, sir, I have mistook;

This is the ring you sent to Silvia. [Shows another ring.]

PROTEUS.

But how cam'st thou by this ring?

At my depart I gave this unto Julia.

JULIA.

And Julia herself did give it me;

And Julia herself have brought it hither.

PROTEUS.

How! Julia!

JULIA.

Behold her that gave aim to all thy oaths,

And entertain'd them deeply in her heart:

How oft hast thou with perjury cleft the root!

O Proteus! let this habit make thee blush.

Be thou asham'd that I have took upon me

Such an immodest raiment; if shame live

In a disguise of love.

It is the lesser blot, modesty finds,

Women to change their shapes than men their minds.

PROTEUS.

Than men their minds! 'tis true. O heaven! were man

But constant, he were perfect: that one error

Fills him with faults; makes him run through all the sins:

Inconstancy falls off ere it begins.

What is in Silvia's face, but I may spy

More fresh in Julia's with a constant eye?

VALENTINE.

Come, come, a hand from either.

Let me be blest to make this happy close;

'Twere pity two such friends should be long foes.

PROTEUS.

Bear witness, heaven, I have my wish for ever.

JULIA.

And I mine.

[Enter OUTLAWS, with DUKE and THURIO.]

OUTLAW.

A prize, a prize, a prize!

VALENTINE.

Forbear, forbear, I say; it is my lord the duke.

Your Grace is welcome to a man disgrac'd,

Banished Valentine.

DUKE.

Sir Valentine!

THURIO.

Yonder is Silvia; and Silvia's mine.

VALENTINE.

Thurio, give back, or else embrace thy death;

Come not within the measure of my wrath;

Do not name Silvia thine; if once again,

Verona shall not hold thee. Here she stands

Take but possession of her with a touch;

I dare thee but to breathe upon my love.

THURIO.

Sir Valentine, I care not for her, I;

I hold him but a fool that will endanger

His body for a girl that loves him not:

I claim her not, and therefore she is thine.

DUKE.

The more degenerate and base art thou

To make such means for her as thou hast done,

And leave her on such slight conditions.

Now, by the honour of my ancestry,

I do applaud thy spirit, Valentine,

And think thee worthy of an empress' love.

Know then, I here forget all former griefs,

Cancel all grudge, repeal thee home again,

Plead a new state in thy unrivall'd merit,

To which I thus subscribe: Sir Valentine,

Thou art a gentleman, and well deriv'd;

Take thou thy Silvia, for thou hast deserv'd her.

VALENTINE.

I thank your Grace; the gift hath made me happy.

I now beseech you, for your daughter's sake,

To grant one boon that I shall ask of you.

DUKE.

I grant it for thine own, whate'er it be.

VALENTINE.

These banish'd men, that I have kept withal,

Are men endu'd with worthy qualities:

Forgive them what they have committed here,

And let them be recall'd from their exile:

They are reformed, civil, full of good,

And fit for great employment, worthy lord.

DUKE.

Thou hast prevail'd; I pardon them, and thee;

Dispose of them as thou know'st their deserts.

Come, let us go; we will include all jars

With triumphs, mirth, and rare solemnity.

VALENTINE.

And, as we walk along, I dare be bold

With our discourse to make your Grace to smile.

What think you of this page, my lord?

DUKE.

I think the boy hath grace in him; he blushes.

VALENTINE.

I warrant you, my lord, more grace than boy.

DUKE.

What mean you by that saying?

VALENTINE.

Please you, I'll tell you as we pass along,

That you will wonder what hath fortuned.

Come, Proteus; 'tis your penance but to hear

The story of your loves discovered:

That done, our day of marriage shall be yours;

One feast, one house, one mutual happiness.

[Exeunt.]

About Author

Shakespeare produced most of his known works between 1589 and 1613. His early plays were primarily comedies and histories and are regarded as some of the best work produced in these genres. Until about 1608, he wrote mainly tragedies, among them Hamlet, Othello, King Lear, and Macbeth, all considered to be among the finest works in the English language. In the last phase of his life, he wrote tragicomedies (also known as romances) and collaborated with other playwrights.

Many of Shakespeare's plays were published in editions of varying quality and accuracy in his lifetime. However, in 1623, two fellow actors and friends of Shakespeare's, John Heminges and Henry Condell, published a more definitive text known as the First Folio, a posthumous collected edition of Shakespeare's dramatic works that included all but two of his plays. The volume was prefaced with a poem by Ben Jonson, in which Jonson presciently hails Shakespeare in a now-famous quote as "not of an age, but for all time".

Throughout the 20th and 21st centuries, Shakespeare's works have been continually adapted and rediscovered by new movements in scholarship and performance. His plays remain popular and are studied, performed, and reinterpreted through various cultural and political contexts around the world.

Early life

William Shakespeare was the son of John Shakespeare, an alderman and a successful glover (glove-maker) originally from Snitterfield, and Mary Arden, the daughter of an affluent landowning farmer. He was born in Stratford-upon-Avon and baptised there on 26 April 1564. His actual date of birth remains unknown, but is traditionally observed on 23 April, Saint George's Day. This date, which can be traced to a mistake made by an 18th-century scholar, has proved appealing to biographers because Shakespeare died on the same date in 1616. He was the third of eight children, and the eldest surviving son.

Although no attendance records for the period survive, most biographers agree that Shakespeare was probably educated at the King's New School in Stratford, a free school chartered in 1553, about a quarter-mile (400 m) from his home. Grammar schools varied in quality during the Elizabethan era, but grammar school curricula were largely similar: the basic Latin text was standardised by royal decree, and the school would have provided an intensive education in grammar based upon Latin classical authors.

At the age of 18, Shakespeare married 26-year-old Anne Hathaway. The consistory court of the Diocese of Worcester issued a marriage licence on 27 November 1582. The next day, two of Hathaway's neighbours posted bonds guaranteeing that no lawful claims impeded the marriage. The ceremony may have been arranged in some haste since the Worcester chancellor allowed the marriage banns to be read once instead of the usual three times, and six months after the marriage Anne gave birth to a daughter, Susanna, baptised 26 May 1583. Twins, son Hamnet and daughter Judith, followed almost two years later and were baptised 2 February 1585. Hamnet died of unknown causes at the age of 11 and was buried 11 August 1596.

After the birth of the twins, Shakespeare left few historical traces until he is mentioned as part of the London theatre scene in 1592. The exception is the appearance of his name in the "complaints bill" of a law case before the Queen's Bench court at Westminster dated Michaelmas Term 1588 and 9 October 1589. Scholars refer to the years between 1585 and 1592 as Shakespeare's "lost years". Biographers attempting to account for this period have reported many apocryphal stories. Nicholas Rowe, Shakespeare's first biographer, recounted a Stratford legend that Shakespeare fled the town for London to escape prosecution for deer poaching in the estate of local squire Thomas Lucy. Shakespeare is also supposed to have taken his revenge on Lucy by writing a scurrilous ballad about him. Another 18th-century story has Shakespeare starting his theatrical career minding the horses of theatre patrons in London. John Aubrey reported that Shakespeare had been a country schoolmaster. Some 20th-century scholars have suggested that Shakespeare may have been employed as a schoolmaster by Alexander

Hoghton of Lancashire, a Catholic landowner who named a certain "William Shakeshafte" in his will. Little evidence substantiates such stories other than hearsay collected after his death, and Shakeshafte was a common name in the Lancashire area.

London and theatrical career

It is not known definitively when Shakespeare began writing, but contemporary allusions and records of performances show that several of his plays were on the London stage by 1592. By then, he was sufficiently known in London to be attacked in print by the playwright Robert Greene in his Groats-Worth of Wit:

... there is an upstart Crow, beautified with our feathers, that with his Tiger's heart wrapped in a Player's hide, supposes he is as well able to bombast out a blank verse as the best of you: and being an absolute Johannes factotum, is in his own conceit the only Shake-scene in a country.

Scholars differ on the exact meaning of Greene's words, but most agree that Greene was accusing Shakespeare of reaching above his rank in trying to match such university-educated writers as Christopher Marlowe, Thomas Nashe, and Greene himself (the so-called "University Wits"). The italicised phrase parodying the line "Oh, tiger's heart wrapped in a woman's hide" from Shakespeare's Henry VI, Part 3, along with the pun "Shake-scene", clearly identify Shakespeare as Greene's target. As used here, Johannes Factotum ("Jack of all trades") refers to a second-rate tinkerer with the work of others, rather than the more common "universal genius".

Greene's attack is the earliest surviving mention of Shakespeare's work in the theatre. Biographers suggest that his career may have begun any time from the mid-1580s to just before Greene's remarks. After 1594, Shakespeare's plays were performed only by the Lord Chamberlain's Men, a company owned by a group of players, including Shakespeare, that soon became the leading playing company in London. After the death of Queen Elizabeth in 1603, the company was awarded a royal patent by the new King James I, and changed its name to the King's Men.

"All the world's a stage,

and all the men and women merely players:

they have their exits and their entrances;

and one man in his time plays many parts ..."

—As You Like It, Act II, Scene 7, 139–142

In 1599, a partnership of members of the company built their own theatre on the south bank of the River Thames, which they named the Globe. In 1608, the partnership also took over the Blackfriars indoor theatre. Extant records of Shakespeare's property purchases and investments indicate that his association with the company made him a wealthy man, and in 1597, he bought the second-largest house in Stratford, New Place, and in 1605, invested in a share of the parish tithes in Stratford.

Some of Shakespeare's plays were published in quarto editions, beginning in 1594, and by 1598, his name had become a selling point and began to appear on the title pages. Shakespeare continued to act in his own and other plays after his success as a playwright. The 1616 edition of Ben Jonson's Works names him on the cast lists for Every Man in His Humour (1598) and Sejanus His Fall (1603). The absence of his name from the 1605 cast list for Jonson's Volpone is taken by some scholars as a sign that his acting career was nearing its end. The First Folio of 1623, however, lists Shakespeare as one of "the Principal Actors in all these Plays", some of which were first staged after Volpone, although we cannot know for certain which roles he played. In 1610, John Davies of Hereford wrote that "good Will" played "kingly" roles. In 1709, Rowe passed down a tradition that Shakespeare played the ghost of Hamlet's father. Later traditions maintain that he also played Adam in As You Like It, and the Chorus in Henry V, though scholars doubt the sources of that information.

Throughout his career, Shakespeare divided his time between London and Stratford. In 1596, the year before he bought New Place as his family home in Stratford, Shakespeare was living in the parish of St. Helen's, Bishopsgate, north of the River Thames. He moved across the river to Southwark by 1599, the same year his company constructed the Globe Theatre there. By 1604, he had moved north of the river again, to an area north of St Paul's Cathedral with many fine houses. There, he rented rooms from a French Huguenot named Christopher Mountjoy, a maker of ladies' wigs and other headgear.

Later years and death

Rowe was the first biographer to record the tradition, repeated by Johnson, that Shakespeare retired to Stratford "some years before his death". He was still working as an actor in London in 1608; in an answer to the sharers' petition in 1635, Cuthbert Burbage stated that after purchasing the lease of the Blackfriars Theatre in 1608 from Henry Evans, the King's Men "placed men players" there, "which were Heminges, Condell, Shakespeare, etc.". However, it is perhaps relevant that the bubonic plague raged in London throughout 1609. The London public playhouses were repeatedly closed during extended outbreaks of the plague (a total of over 60 months closure between May 1603 and February 1610), which meant there was often no acting work. Retirement from all work was uncommon at that time. Shakespeare continued to visit London during the years 1611–1614. In 1612, he was called as a witness in Bellott v. Mountjoy, a court case concerning the marriage settlement of Mountjoy's daughter, Mary. In March 1613, he bought a gatehouse in the former Blackfriars priory; and from November 1614, he was in London for several weeks with his son-in-law, John Hall. After 1610, Shakespeare wrote fewer plays, and none are attributed to him after 1613. His last three plays were collaborations, probably with John Fletcher, who succeeded him as the house playwright of the King's Men.

Shakespeare died on 23 April 1616, at the age of 52. He died within a month of signing his will, a document which he begins by describing himself as being in "perfect health". No extant contemporary source explains how or why he died. Half a century later, John Ward, the vicar of Stratford, wrote in his notebook: "Shakespeare, Drayton, and Ben Jonson had a merry meeting and, it seems, drank too hard, for Shakespeare died of a fever there contracted", not an impossible scenario since Shakespeare knew Jonson and Drayton. Of the tributes from fellow authors, one refers to his relatively sudden death: "We wondered, Shakespeare, that thou went'st so soon / From

155

the world's stage to the grave's tiring room."

He was survived by his wife and two daughters. Susanna had married a physician, John Hall, in 1607, and Judith had married Thomas Quiney, a vintner, two months before Shakespeare's death. Shakespeare signed his last will and testament on 25 March 1616; the following day, his new son-in-law, Thomas Quiney was found guilty of fathering an illegitimate son by Margaret Wheeler, who had died during childbirth. Thomas was ordered by the church court to do public penance, which would have caused much shame and embarrassment for the Shakespeare family.

Shakespeare bequeathed the bulk of his large estate to his elder daughter Susanna under stipulations that she pass it down intact to "the first son of her body". The Quineys had three children, all of whom died without marrying. The Halls had one child, Elizabeth, who married twice but died without children in 1670, ending Shakespeare's direct line. Shakespeare's will scarcely mentions his wife, Anne, who was probably entitled to one-third of his estate automatically. He did make a point, however, of leaving her "my second best bed", a bequest that has led to much speculation. Some scholars see the bequest as an insult to Anne, whereas others believe that the second-best bed would have been the matrimonial bed and therefore rich in significance.

Shakespeare was buried in the chancel of the Holy Trinity Church two days after his death. The epitaph carved into the stone slab covering his grave includes a curse against moving his bones, which was carefully avoided during restoration of the church in 2008:

Good frend for Iesvs sake forbeare,

To digg the dvst enclosed heare.

Bleste be Middle English the.svg man Middle English that.svg spares thes stones,

And cvrst be he Middle English that.svg moves my bones.

(Modern spelling: Good friend, for Jesus' sake forbear, / To dig the dust enclosed here. / Blessed be the man that spares these stones, / And cursed be

156

he that moves my bones.)

Some time before 1623, a funerary monument was erected in his memory on the north wall, with a half-effigy of him in the act of writing. Its plaque compares him to Nestor, Socrates, and Virgil. In 1623, in conjunction with the publication of the First Folio, the Droeshout engraving was published.

Shakespeare has been commemorated in many statues and memorials around the world, including funeral monuments in Southwark Cathedral and Poets' Corner in Westminster Abbey.

Plays

Most playwrights of the period typically collaborated with others at some point, and critics agree that Shakespeare did the same, mostly early and late in his career. Some attributions, such as Titus Andronicus and the early history plays, remain controversial while The Two Noble Kinsmen and the lost Cardenio have well-attested contemporary documentation. Textual evidence also supports the view that several of the plays were revised by other writers after their original composition.

The first recorded works of Shakespeare are Richard III and the three parts of Henry VI, written in the early 1590s during a vogue for historical drama. Shakespeare's plays are difficult to date precisely, however, and studies of the texts suggest that Titus Andronicus, The Comedy of Errors, The Taming of the Shrew, and The Two Gentlemen of Verona may also belong to Shakespeare's earliest period. His first histories, which draw heavily on the 1587 edition of Raphael Holinshed's Chronicles of England, Scotland, and Ireland, dramatise the destructive results of weak or corrupt rule and have been interpreted as a justification for the origins of the Tudor dynasty. The early plays were influenced by the works of other Elizabethan dramatists, especially Thomas Kyd and Christopher Marlowe, by the traditions of medieval drama, and by the plays of Seneca. The Comedy of Errors was also based on classical models, but no source for The Taming of the Shrew has been found, though it is related to a separate play of the same name and may have derived from a folk story. Like The Two Gentlemen of Verona, in which two friends appear to approve of rape, the Shrew's story of the taming of a woman's independent spirit by a man sometimes troubles modern critics, directors, and audiences.

Shakespeare's early classical and Italianate comedies, containing tight double plots and precise comic sequences, give way in the mid-1590s to the romantic atmosphere of his most acclaimed comedies. A Midsummer Night's Dream is a witty mixture of romance, fairy magic, and comic lowlife scenes. Shakespeare's next comedy, the equally romantic Merchant of Venice, contains a portrayal of the vengeful Jewish moneylender Shylock, which reflects Elizabethan views but may appear derogatory to modern audiences. The wit and wordplay of Much Ado About Nothing, the charming rural setting of As You Like It, and the lively merrymaking of Twelfth Night complete Shakespeare's sequence of great comedies. After the lyrical Richard II, written almost entirely in verse, Shakespeare introduced prose comedy into the histories of the late 1590s, Henry IV, parts 1 and 2, and Henry V. His characters become more complex and tender as he switches deftly between comic and serious scenes, prose and poetry, and achieves the narrative variety of his mature work. This period begins and ends with two tragedies: Romeo and Juliet, the famous romantic tragedy of sexually charged adolescence, love, and death; and Julius Caesar—based on Sir Thomas North's 1579 translation of Plutarch's Parallel Lives—which introduced a new kind of drama. According to Shakespearean scholar James Shapiro, in Julius Caesar, "the various strands of politics, character, inwardness, contemporary events, even Shakespeare's own reflections on the act of writing, began to infuse each other".

In the early 17th century, Shakespeare wrote the so-called "problem plays" Measure for Measure, Troilus and Cressida, and All's Well That Ends Well and a number of his best known tragedies. Many critics believe that Shakespeare's greatest tragedies represent the peak of his art. The titular hero of one of Shakespeare's greatest tragedies, Hamlet, has probably been discussed more than any other Shakespearean character, especially for his famous soliloquy which begins "To be or not to be; that is the question". Unlike the introverted Hamlet, whose fatal flaw is hesitation, the heroes of the tragedies that followed, Othello and King Lear, are undone by hasty errors of judgement. The plots of Shakespeare's tragedies often hinge on such fatal errors or flaws, which overturn order and destroy the hero and those he loves. In Othello, the villain Iago stokes Othello's sexual jealousy to the point where he murders the innocent wife who loves him. In King Lear, the old king commits the tragic error of giving up his powers, initiating the events which lead to the torture and blinding of the Earl of Gloucester and the murder of Lear's youngest daughter Cordelia. According to the critic Frank Kermode, "the play-offers neither its good characters nor its audience any relief from its cruelty". In Macbeth, the shortest and most compressed of Shakespeare's tragedies, uncontrollable ambition incites Macbeth and his wife, Lady Macbeth, to murder the rightful king and usurp the throne until their own guilt destroys them in turn. In this play, Shakespeare adds a supernatural element to the tragic structure. His last major tragedies, Antony and Cleopatra and Coriolanus, contain some of Shakespeare's finest poetry and were considered his most successful tragedies by the poet and critic T.S. Eliot.

In his final period, Shakespeare turned to romance or tragicomedy and completed three more major plays: Cymbeline, The Winter's Tale, and The Tempest, as well as the collaboration, Pericles, Prince of Tyre. Less bleak than the tragedies, these four plays are graver in tone than the comedies of the 1590s, but they end with reconciliation and the forgiveness of potentially tragic errors. Some commentators have seen this change in mood as evidence of a more serene view of life on Shakespeare's part, but it may merely reflect the theatrical fashion of the day. Shakespeare collaborated on two further surviving plays, Henry VIII and The Two Noble Kinsmen, probably with John Fletcher.

Performances

It is not clear for which companies Shakespeare wrote his early plays. The title page of the 1594 edition of Titus Andronicus reveals that the play had been acted by three different troupes. After the plagues of 1592–3, Shakespeare's plays were performed by his own company at The Theatre and the Curtain in Shoreditch, north of the Thames. Londoners flocked there to see the first part of Henry IV, Leonard Digges recording, "Let but Falstaff come, Hal, Poins, the rest ... and you scarce shall have a room". When the company found themselves in dispute with their landlord, they pulled The

Theatre down and used the timbers to construct the Globe Theatre, the first playhouse built by actors for actors, on the south bank of the Thames at Southwark. The Globe opened in autumn 1599, with Julius Caesar one of the first plays staged. Most of Shakespeare's greatest post-1599 plays were written for the Globe, including Hamlet, Othello, and King Lear.

After the Lord Chamberlain's Men were renamed the King's Men in 1603, they entered a special relationship with the new King James. Although the performance records are patchy, the King's Men performed seven of Shakespeare's plays at court between 1 November 1604, and 31 October 1605, including two performances of The Merchant of Venice. After 1608, they performed at the indoor Blackfriars Theatre during the winter and the Globe during the summer. The indoor setting, combined with the Jacobean fashion for lavishly staged masques, allowed Shakespeare to introduce more elaborate stage devices. In Cymbeline, for example, Jupiter descends "in thunder and lightning, sitting upon an eagle: he throws a thunderbolt. The ghosts fall on their knees."

The actors in Shakespeare's company included the famous Richard Burbage, William Kempe, Henry Condell and John Heminges. Burbage played the leading role in the first performances of many of Shakespeare's plays, including Richard III, Hamlet, Othello, and King Lear. The popular comic actor Will Kempe played the servant Peter in Romeo and Juliet and Dogberry in Much Ado About Nothing, among other characters. He was replaced around 1600 by Robert Armin, who played roles such as Touchstone in As You Like It and the fool in King Lear. In 1613, Sir Henry Wotton recorded that Henry VIII "was set forth with many extraordinary circumstances of pomp and ceremony". On 29 June, however, a cannon set fire to the thatch of the Globe and burned the theatre to the ground, an event which pinpoints the date of a Shakespeare play with rare precision.

Textual sources

In 1623, John Heminges and Henry Condell, two of Shakespeare's friends from the King's Men, published the First Folio, a collected edition of Shakespeare's plays. It contained 36 texts, including 18 printed for the first time. Many of the plays had already appeared in quarto versions—flimsy books made from sheets of paper folded twice to make four leaves. No evidence suggests that Shakespeare approved these editions, which the First Folio describes as "stol'n and surreptitious copies". Nor did Shakespeare plan or expect his works to survive in any form at all; those works likely would have faded into oblivion but for his friends' spontaneous idea, after his death, to create and publish the First Folio.

Alfred Pollard termed some of the pre-1623 versions as "bad quartos" because of their adapted, paraphrased or garbled texts, which may in places have been reconstructed from memory. Where several versions of a play survive, each differs from the other. The differences may stem from copying or printing errors, from notes by actors or audience members, or from Shakespeare's own papers. In some cases, for example, Hamlet, Troilus and Cressida, and Othello, Shakespeare could have revised the texts between the quarto and folio editions. In the case of King Lear, however, while most modern editions do conflate them, the 1623 folio version is so different from the 1608 quarto that the Oxford Shakespeare prints them both, arguing that they cannot be conflated without confusion.

Influence from neighbours in London

Ten years of research by Geoffrey Marsh (museum director) of the Victoria and Albert Museum in London may have shown that Shakespeare got many of the ideas and information for his plays, from his neighbours that he lived near in London in the late 1590s.

Geoffrey Marsh found the site of Shakespeare's house in St Helen's Church, Bishopsgate parish, at the corner of St.Helen's churchyard and Bishopsgate Street, north of the churchyard, from the records of the Leathersellers Company. Many wealthy and notable people (including Sir John Spencer and Dr. Edward Jorden and Dr. Peter Turner), with connections across Europe, lived near Shakespeare.

Poems

In 1593 and 1594, when the theatres were closed because of plague,

Shakespeare published two narrative poems on sexual themes, Venus and Adonis and The Rape of Lucrece. He dedicated them to Henry Wriothesley, Earl of Southampton. In Venus and Adonis, an innocent Adonis rejects the sexual advances of Venus; while in The Rape of Lucrece, the virtuous wife Lucrece is raped by the lustful Tarquin. Influenced by Ovid's Metamorphoses, the poems show the guilt and moral confusion that result from uncontrolled lust. Both proved popular and were often reprinted during Shakespeare's lifetime. A third narrative poem, A Lover's Complaint, in which a young woman laments her seduction by a persuasive suitor, was printed in the first edition of the Sonnets in 1609. Most scholars now accept that Shakespeare wrote A Lover's Complaint. Critics consider that its fine qualities are marred by leaden effects. The Phoenix and the Turtle, printed in Robert Chester's 1601 Love's Martyr, mourns the deaths of the legendary phoenix and his lover, the faithful turtle dove. In 1599, two early drafts of sonnets 138 and 144 appeared in The Passionate Pilgrim, published under Shakespeare's name but without his permission.

Sonnets

Published in 1609, the Sonnets were the last of Shakespeare's non-dramatic works to be printed. Scholars are not certain when each of the 154 sonnets was composed, but evidence suggests that Shakespeare wrote sonnets throughout his career for a private readership. Even before the two unauthorised sonnets appeared in The Passionate Pilgrim in 1599, Francis Meres had referred in 1598 to Shakespeare's "sugred Sonnets among his private friends". Few analysts believe that the published collection follows Shakespeare's intended sequence. He seems to have planned two contrasting series: one about uncontrollable lust for a married woman of dark complexion (the "dark lady"), and one about conflicted love for a fair young man (the "fair youth"). It remains unclear if these figures represent real individuals, or if the authorial "I" who addresses them represents Shakespeare himself, though Wordsworth believed that with the sonnets "Shakespeare unlocked his heart".

"Shall I compare thee to a summer's day?

Thou art more lovely and more temperate ..."

—Lines from Shakespeare's Sonnet 18.

The 1609 edition was dedicated to a "Mr. W.H.", credited as "the only begetter" of the poems. It is not known whether this was written by Shakespeare himself or by the publisher, Thomas Thorpe, whose initials appear at the foot of the dedication page; nor is it known who Mr. W.H. was, despite numerous theories, or whether Shakespeare even authorised the publication. Critics praise the Sonnets as a profound meditation on the nature of love, sexual passion, procreation, death, and time.

Style

Shakespeare's first plays were written in the conventional style of the day. He wrote them in a stylised language that does not always spring naturally from the needs of the characters or the drama. The poetry depends on extended, sometimes elaborate metaphors and conceits, and the language is often rhetorical—written for actors to declaim rather than speak. The grand speeches in Titus Andronicus, in the view of some critics, often hold up the action, for example; and the verse in The Two Gentlemen of Verona has been described as stilted.

However, Shakespeare soon began to adapt the traditional styles to his own purposes. The opening soliloquy of Richard III has its roots in the self-declaration of Vice in medieval drama. At the same time, Richard's vivid self-awareness looks forward to the soliloquies of Shakespeare's mature plays. No single play marks a change from the traditional to the freer style. Shakespeare combined the two throughout his career, with Romeo and Juliet perhaps the best example of the mixing of the styles. By the time of Romeo and Juliet, Richard II, and A Midsummer Night's Dream in the mid-1590s, Shakespeare had begun to write a more natural poetry. He increasingly tuned his metaphors and images to the needs of the drama itself.

Shakespeare's standard poetic form was blank verse, composed in iambic pentameter. In practice, this meant that his verse was usually unrhymed and consisted of ten syllables to a line, spoken with a stress on every second syllable. The blank verse of his early plays is quite different from that of his later ones. It is often beautiful, but its sentences tend to start, pause, and finish at the end of lines, with the risk of monotony. Once Shakespeare mastered traditional blank verse, he began to interrupt and vary its flow. This technique releases the new power and flexibility of the poetry in plays such as Julius Caesar and Hamlet. Shakespeare uses it, for example, to convey the turmoil in Hamlet's mind:

Sir, in my heart there was a kind of fighting

That would not let me sleep. Methought I lay

Worse than the mutines in the bilboes. Rashly—

And prais'd be rashness for it—let us know

Our indiscretion sometimes serves us well ...

—Hamlet, Act 5, Scene 2, 4–8

After Hamlet, Shakespeare varied his poetic style further, particularly in the more emotional passages of the late tragedies. The literary critic A. C. Bradley described this style as "more concentrated, rapid, varied, and, in construction, less regular, not seldom twisted or elliptical". In the last phase of his career, Shakespeare adopted many techniques to achieve these effects. These included run-on lines, irregular pauses and stops, and extreme variations in sentence structure and length. In Macbeth, for example, the language darts from one unrelated metaphor or simile to another: "was the hope drunk/ Wherein you dressed yourself?" (1.7.35–38); "... pity, like a naked new-born babe/ Striding the blast, or heaven's cherubim, hors'd/ Upon the sightless couriers of the air ..." (1.7.21–25). The listener is challenged to complete the sense. The late romances, with their shifts in time and surprising turns of plot, inspired a last poetic style in which long and short sentences are set against one another, clauses are piled up, subject and object are reversed, and words are omitted, creating an effect of spontaneity.

Shakespeare combined poetic genius with a practical sense of the theatre. Like all playwrights of the time, he dramatised stories from sources such as Plutarch and Holinshed. He reshaped each plot to create several centres of interest and to show as many sides of a narrative to the audience as possible. This strength of design ensures that a Shakespeare play can survive translation, cutting and wide interpretation without loss to its core drama. As Shakespeare's mastery grew, he gave his characters clearer and more varied motivations and distinctive patterns of speech. He preserved aspects of his earlier style in the later plays, however. In Shakespeare's late romances, he deliberately returned to a more artificial style, which emphasised the illusion of theatre.

Influence

Shakespeare's work has made a lasting impression on later theatre and literature. In particular, he expanded the dramatic potential of characterisation, plot, language, and genre. Until Romeo and Juliet, for example, romance had not been viewed as a worthy topic for tragedy. Soliloquies had been used mainly to convey information about characters or events, but Shakespeare used them to explore characters' minds. His work heavily influenced later poetry. The Romantic poets attempted to revive Shakespearean verse drama, though with little success. Critic George Steiner described all English verse dramas from Coleridge to Tennyson as "feeble variations on Shakespearean themes."

Shakespeare influenced novelists such as Thomas Hardy, William Faulkner, and Charles Dickens. The American novelist Herman Melville's soliloquies owe much to Shakespeare; his Captain Ahab in Moby-Dick is a classic tragic hero, inspired by King Lear. Scholars have identified 20,000 pieces of music linked to Shakespeare's works. These include three operas by Giuseppe Verdi, Macbeth, Otello and Falstaff, whose critical standing compares with that of the source plays. Shakespeare has also inspired many painters, including the Romantics and the Pre-Raphaelites. The Swiss Romantic artist Henry Fuseli, a friend of William Blake, even translated Macbeth into German. The psychoanalyst Sigmund Freud drew on Shakespearean psychology, in particular, that of Hamlet, for his theories of human nature.

In Shakespeare's day, English grammar, spelling, and pronunciation were less standardised than they are now, and his use of language helped shape modern English. Samuel Johnson quoted him more often than any other author in his A Dictionary of the English Language, the first serious work of its type. Expressions such as "with bated breath" (Merchant of Venice) and "a foregone conclusion" (Othello) have found their way into everyday English speech.

Works

Classification of the plays

Shakespeare's works include the 36 plays printed in the First Folio of 1623, listed according to their folio classification as comedies, histories, and tragedies. Two plays not included in the First Folio, The Two Noble Kinsmen and Pericles, Prince of Tyre, are now accepted as part of the canon, with today's scholars agreeing that Shakespeare made major contributions to the writing of both. No Shakespearean poems were included in the First Folio.

In the late 19th century, Edward Dowden classified four of the late comedies as romances, and though many scholars prefer to call them tragicomedies, Dowden's term is often used. In 1896, Frederick S. Boas coined the term "problem plays" to describe four plays: All's Well That Ends Well, Measure for Measure, Troilus and Cressida, and Hamlet. "Dramas as singular in theme and temper cannot be strictly called comedies or tragedies", he wrote. "We may, therefore, borrow a convenient phrase from the theatre of today and class them together as Shakespeare's problem plays." The term, much debated and sometimes applied to other plays, remains in use, though Hamlet is definitively classed as a tragedy. (Source: Wikipedia)

Printed in July 2019
by Rotomail Italia S.p.A., Vignate (MI) - Italy